Bryan's book is the best guide _____
respond to God's abounding l _____
offers the extravagant devoti _____
immeasurably blessed.
Robert Morris, Senior Pastor
Gateway Church—Southlake, TX
Author of *The Blessed Life*

Church leaders take note: Bryan Jarrett's Extravagant
can set your people on fire for God! The remarkable
personal story—and equally remarkable principles— he
shares about what God does when we respond to Him
extravagantly just might revolutionize your spiritual
life—and your church.
George Wood, General Superintendent
Assemblies of God USA—Springfield, MO
Author of *Roadtrip Leadership*

If ever there was a wake-up call to point Christians
toward a deeper, more exciting experience of God, Bryan
Jarrett's book is it. The revolutionary discipleship he
reveals in Extravagant *is irresistible.*
Matthew Barnett, President, The Dream Center
and Senior Pastor, Angelus Temple—Los Angeles, CA
Author of *The Church that Never Sleeps*

EXTRAVAGANT! Since the first time I met Pastor Bryan
Jarrett there was an extravagance about him. As a pastor,
his vision was extravagant. As a father, his devotion to
his children was extravagant. As a husband, his untiring
love for his wife was extravagant. It is no surprise that
this book is titled Extravagant! An extravagant God
loving us extravagantly—beyond reasonable limits,
unrestrained and overabundant. If that is what you want
to experience, then this book is for you. Read and start
living the extravagant life now!
Dr. Samuel R. Chand
Author of *Cracking Your Church's Culture Code*
(www.samchand.com)

bryan jarrett

foreword by **mark batterson**

living out **Your** *response to* **God's** outrageous love

 Influence

www.InfluenceResources.com

Published by Influence Resources
1445 N. Boonville Ave., Springfield, Missouri 65802

Published in association with The Quadrivium Group—Orlando, FL
info@TheQuadriviumGroup.com
and New Vantage Partners—Franklin, TN
info@NewVantagePartners.net

Cover and interior design by Allen Creative—Snellville, GA
Typesetting by Wellspring Design and Jay Victor—Nashville, TN

ISBN: 978-1-936699-11-7

First printing 2011

Printed in United States of America

Both of my father figures were alive when I started this project.
Both made it to heaven before its completion.
I dedicate this book to my maternal grandfather,
M.D. Gibson, and my father, **Roy Jarrett:**

To my grandfather, who was the father he didn't have to be;
And to my father, who became the father he never was.

contents

acknowledgements

Thank you, **Jesus**! The only reason I have the capacity to understand extravagance is that You initiated love and pursued me with "unrestrained excess."

Extravagant devotion is modeled every day in my home by the way **Haley** and **my three children** love me. Your love provides the safe place for me to be who God has called me to be.

Thank you to the **two congregations** that have given me the honor of being called "Pastor."

First Assembly of God in Pine Bluff, Arkansas, you gave an unproven 25-year-old preacher a chance to pastor a 75-year-old church with rich tradition. Your love, patience, and willingness to follow me into crazy leaps of faith will inspire me for the rest of my life.

Northplace Church, thank you for being a laboratory for New Testament Christianity to be on display to a 21st century world. Thank you for your Kingdom-mindedness, for it has liberated me to pursue the unique call on my life. Apart from Jesus and my family, you are the love of my life.

To our **staff,** your competence makes the dream possible, your extravagance brings honor to God, and your friendship makes the journey worthwhile.

To **Dr. George Wood,** thank you for your vision of creating a platform for Spirit-filled authors to impact the world.

To **Pat Springle,** thank you for letting me stand on your shoulders in the writing process. This would not have been possible without you.

To my editors who became so much more: **David Shepherd** and **Greg Webster.** Your dedication to the message of this book manifested itself in your excellence in the process. Your professionalism and wisdom made the project better, and knowing you has made me better.

To **Steve and Susan Blount,** you have mentored a first time author through this process with great care. Thank you for sharing your years of experience with me.

foreword

February 6th has always been a special date for my family. It's my youngest son's birthday. This year Josiah turned nine, and one of the greatest dreams of his young life came true on that very day. He watched our family's favorite team, the Green Bay Packers, win Super Bowl XLV—in person. It'll be tough to top that gift! But I'm not the father who "spoiled" my son by taking him to the Super Bowl as a birthday present. No, the dad who did that was Bryan Jarrett, a man who allowed himself to be used by our mutual Father in heaven to lavish an inexpressibly memorable experience on a little boy He and I both love.

Our trip to the Super Bowl started three weeks before the big event. On Monday morning after the Packers had clinched their spot, I sent out a light-hearted "Tweet" about my son's birthday falling on the day the Packers would play in the Super Bowl. Seeing an opportunity, Bryan called from his church in Dallas to say he wanted to buy my son and me tickets to the Super Bowl and give us an expense-paid trip to the championship game. There was only one catch—and in light of the immensity of his offer, it was truly a very small one. Pastor Bryan wanted me to preach at his church on Super Bowl Sunday. It took me less than a nanosecond to decide that rearranging my schedule was worth that price.

Bryan's present was beyond extravagant. His church's love offering paid every penny for our trip to Dallas and the game. As I look back, it's no wonder. His church is accustomed to outrageous generosity because it's a church Bryan has introduced intimately to a God who will stop at nothing to love His people. They've learned their extravagance from the Original Extravagant One.

The story of how God progressively introduced Bryan to His extravagant love reads like an unbelievably great novel. You can't guess what God will do next. Bryan couldn't. And like me, I'm sure you'll relish seeing how the nature of God's extravagance elevates human devotion to remarkable levels.

I share some experiences in common with Bryan. We attended the same seminary (a few years apart). We're both pastors, and we talk now and then about sermon ideas and leadership challenges. Over the last few years I've come to respect Bryan as a gifted leader and humble man of God. His passion for the Lord is contagious, as is his willingness to go out on a limb for God. After reading this book, you'll want to go out on a limb, too! I know I do.

Mark Batterson
Lead Pastor—National Community Church
Washington, DC
June 2011

introduction

extravagant by nature

Who comes to mind when you think of the world's wealthiest people? Warren Buffet? Bill Gates? Your great uncle (wouldn't that be nice)? Whoever it might be, the lavish riches at their disposal are unimaginable to most of us. And in many cases, the level of generosity of which they're capable is beyond what we could give away in a hundred lifetimes at whatever our current income level may be. Yet, if you were to compile the tens of billions of dollars in net worth of one of these people, every penny they have would not be enough to match the donation made by one man in the Bible to the work God called him to.

Before he died, David, the second king of Israel, wanted nothing more than to be the person to build a temple to the God to whom he had given his whole heart for most of his eighty years. Ever the obedient servant, he begged the Lord to release him to the task, but God turned him down. Instead, David's Lord decreed that the king's son, Solomon, would be the one honored with the job of constructing a house for the one true God. Yet God's re-direction did not dissuade David from his vision to see a temple built. No, he became all the more determined to guarantee the success of the project. He created a plan to make sure Solomon had everything he needed to build a temple that would outshine all others. So David made a donation and with it gave Solomon these instructions:

I have taken great pains to provide for the temple of the Lord a hundred thousand talents of gold, a million talents of silver, quantities of bronze and iron too great to be weighed, and wood and stone. And you may add to them. You have many workmen: stonecutters, masons and carpenters, as well as men skilled in every kind of work in gold and silver, bronze and iron—craftsmen beyond number. Now begin the work, and the Lord be with you. (1 Chronicles 22:14-16)

Let's put these quantities into modern terms, just so you'll have a perspective on the overwhelming size of David's gift. A talent of metal weighed about 70 pounds. That means David gave roughly 3750 *tons* of gold or about 7.5 million pounds. Multiply that by 16 to get the number of ounces, and based on today's price per ounce, David's gold donation alone was worth about $180 *billion*. Add to that his 37,500 *tons* of silver worth today about $42 billion, and even without considering the other materials given, you come up with an offering that is three or four times larger than the *entire fortune* of one of today's richest people. We don't know how much David had left for himself after giving it, but his was undoubtedly the largest donation to anything in history.

What in the world could possibly motivate such extravagance?

I believe it was David's crystal clear recognition that every single thing—every shekel, every cow, every sandal, every fringe on his garment—had come to him from the hand of God, and it was only right to give back lavishly as a demonstration of his gratitude. While I can't say whether or not it was an easy thing for David to give so much, I can say that his response to God was completely natural for one

2

so in touch with his heavenly Father. We are extravagant in our response to God because He is extravagant by nature.

When people think of "the nature of God," theologically correct ideas come to mind: God is love; God is just; God is holy. And they're all true. But we miss something by not recognizing the superlatives that go with each of those descriptions of His nature. The angel in Isaiah's vision cried, "Holy, holy, holy!"—an extreme exclamation. "Holy" by itself is already perfect, sinless, pure, righteous. But the angel felt compelled to shout it three times for emphasis. That's because God isn't just kind of holy or kind of loving or kind of just. He is lavishly, immoderately, abundantly, excessively, sumptuously, bountifully, prolifically holy, loving, and just in every iota of His infinite being. God is, in a word, extravagant. His very being is extravagant. The extent of his every quality is limitless.

> We are extravagant in our response to God because He is extravagant by nature.

It is this extravagant reality of God that King David responded to. The closer a person walks with the Almighty, the clearer His extravagance registers in our consciousness. And when it does, it unleashes in our hearts and minds an extravagance of devotion that transforms life into an experience inconceivable to anyone who hasn't yet "gotten it."

It's this experience of an extravagant God that I hope to draw you into with this book. David is only one example of people in the Bible who "got it." I'll point out some others. I've also dipped my toe in this water of God's extravagance and have some stories of my own journey that I hope will encourage you to see that the "extravagance cycle"—God is extravagant to us, which triggers an extravagant response

3

from us, which prompts further expressions of extravagance from God—is as real today as it was in 1000 B.C. when David was king.

In this book, I'm neither calling people to a vow of poverty nor to an expectation that God will flood material riches their way. There's nothing particularly holy about being poor, and there's nothing biblically guaranteed about getting rich. We can be sold out to God whether we are wealthy or indigent. A heart of extravagance can be demonstrated by people in the penthouse as well as in the poorhouse. My purpose is to call you to make a radical, dramatic, complete commitment to Him in response to the outpouring of God's immense love for you.

> We can be sold out to God whether we are wealthy or indigent.

A heart revolution changes how we view our possessions, positions, and relationships and will teach us to define "rich" in a very different way than the world does. In his riveting book, *The Pursuit of God,* A. W. Tozer explains "the blessedness of possessing nothing":

> *Our woes began when God was forced out of His central shrine and "things" were allowed to enter. Within the human heart "things" have taken over. Men have now by nature no peace within their hearts, for God is crowned there no longer, but there in the moral dusk stubborn and aggressive usurpers fight among themselves for first place on the throne. . . . Let me exhort you to take this seriously. It is not to be understood as mere Bible teaching to be stored away in the mind along with an inert mass of other doctrines.*

4

*It is a marker on the road to greener pastures,
a path chiseled against the steep sides of the
mount of God. We dare not try to by-pass it if we
would follow on in this holy pursuit. We must
ascend a step at a time. If we refuse one step we
bring our progress to an end.* [1]

If I encourage you to take a single step, and then another
and another, I'll be satisfied that this book has done its job.
With just one hint of God's extravagance, living your own
life of extravagant devotion will become irresistible.

5

---

1. A. W. Tozer, *The Pursuit of God* (CreateSpace, 2010), 18.

a word from the wise

Solomon got the message. His father's over-the-top devotion to God captured the young king's heart, and he responded through his own life of lavish commitment to the Lord.

When Solomon came to the throne, he inherited a united empire. David's wars had brought peace to the land—and heavy responsibility to Solomon's shoulders. A conscientious leader, Solomon knew his limitations and determined to make sure he would not let anyone down—not the people of Israel, not his father on earth, not his Father in heaven. So he turned first to the Father whose plan for world history and Solomon personally had put him on the throne.

According to Scripture, Solomon sought the Lord by offering sacrifices of praise at Gibeon. While there, the Lord appeared to him in a dream and made him a remarkable offer: "Ask for whatever you want me to give you" (1 Kings 3:5).

The third king of Israel could have asked for military might, fabulous wealth, or political fame, but instead, he asked God to give him wisdom so he could adequately lead his people:

> *Now, O Lord my God, you have made your servant king in place of my father David. But I am only a little child and do not know how to carry out my duties. Your servant is here among the people you have chosen, a great people, too nu-*

merous to count or number. So give your servant a discerning heart to govern your people and to distinguish between right and wrong. For who is able to govern this great people of yours? (1 Kings 3:7-9)

Solomon's request thrilled God's heart. In response to the king's humility, God gave him uncommon spiritual wisdom, but, in addition, He also gave him fabulous wealth and honor among the nations.

In keeping with his father David's wishes, Solomon made plans to build a temple that would be a marvel of beauty and architecture. Workmen brought the finest cedar logs from Lebanon. Craftsmen sculpted the billions' worth of gold and silver. Men quarried blocks of marble so skillfully that construction workers didn't need hammers and chisels to fit the stones together at the building site.

When the temple was complete, Solomon sponsored an elaborate dedication service. Priests carried the ark of the covenant into the Holy of Holies, and a cloud filled the temple with God's presence. Solomon offered a prayer of dedication and then provided an enormous sacrifice on the new altar. He "offered a sacrifice of fellowship offerings to the Lord: twenty-two thousand cattle and a hundred and twenty thousand sheep and goats. So the king and all the Israelites dedicated the temple of the Lord" (1 Kings 8:63).

We have a hard time grasping the significance of the moment. What are the sounds, smells, and sights of sacrificing 142,000 animals in a colossal worship service? This was, to be sure, an extravagant display of worship by Solomon and his people for the goodness of God in establishing their nation, giving them a home, and guiding them uniquely among all people. The Lord hadn't commanded Solomon to sacrifice so much. It was simply the overflow of his intense gratitude for all God had done for him and his people. And

God kept the cycle going. In response, He opened heaven's storehouse to honor the one who honored him. Back and forth God and Solomon went: Solomon honoring God, God rewarding the king, and the king humbly praising God and trusting Him for further guidance.

Some of us might think, "Well, that's fine for David and Solomon to offer such extravagant gifts. They were rich kings and could afford it." The language of extravagance, though, isn't a dialect reserved for the wealthy and social elite. Jesus made clear that *anyone* can live this kind of extraordinary life and communicate with God in this way. Mark's gospel takes us to a scene during the last week before Jesus' crucifixion:

> **Anyone can live this extraordinary life and communicate with God in this way.**

> *Jesus sat down opposite the place where the offerings were put and watched the crowd putting their money into the temple treasury. Many rich people threw in large amounts. But a poor widow came and put in two very small copper coins, worth only a fraction of a penny. Calling His disciples to Him, Jesus said, "I tell you the truth, this poor widow has put more into the treasury than all the others. They all gave out of their wealth; but she, out of her poverty, put in everything—all she had to live on." (Mark 12:41-44)*

Why did this poor woman give everything to God? Because she had a heart of overwhelming gratitude and glad obedience. And how much was her gift worth to Jesus? Enough for Him to point to her as a shining example for all of us. This woman was a thoroughly forgettable historical figure and an insignificant visitor to the temple—*until her extravagance captured God's heart*. Jesus noticed her, and because her unsparing gift attracted His attention, she will never be forgotten. Throughout the Scriptures, we see that lives of extravagant devotion and surrender to Him captured the heart of God. And they still do.

Calling God's Bluff

I began to learn about the importance of such devotion when I first became a Christian at age seven (more about that later), but the Lord took me to a new level of understanding a few years into a ministry through which I thought I had already come to understand a lot about the workings of God. How little I really knew!

At the time, I was a young (*really* young—I started preaching at age 16!) evangelist traveling around the country speaking at church revivals and other events. Several years into a remarkably "successful" ministry, my young wife and co-ministry enthusiast, Haley, and I were driving to our next engagement, in Clinton, Mississippi, between Memphis, Tennessee and Jackson, Mississippi. Haley was asleep beside me in the car when I heard the Lord whisper, "Bryan, surrender."

I figured He must have wandered into the wrong car. His direction was certainly intended for someone else. My less-than-instantly obedient response was, "Lord, what else do You want me to surrender? I've already given enough!"

After all, I had planned on being a doctor but gave up that "worldly ambition" to become an evangelist. I had dreamed of going into medicine specifically so I could have a more well-to-do life than anyone in my family had ever enjoyed. If I could go to medical school and become a physician, I'd thought, I would have it made! I'd really be somebody. I'd have proven that I was someone with special skills and intelligence. I would be admired in our society. But when I answered God's call to be an evangelist, I knew exactly what *that* meant—meager pay, worry about money for bills, and perhaps worst of all, being one of "those" people.

With all that in mind, I was more than a little resentful when God whispered to me on the road that night, but He took my response in stride. "Bryan," the Lord continued, "in reality, you don't know much about surrender, but I'm going to teach you about it for the rest of your life." I'm not sure that's what I wanted to hear, but God was true to His word.

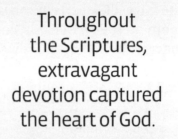

Throughout the Scriptures, extravagant devotion captured the heart of God.

Even though I'm writing this book, I'm still very much learning, and I have a long way to go. I feel like Winston Churchill after the British victory over the German Afrika Korps at the Second Battle of El Alamein in Egypt. He famously reflected, "Now this is not the end. It is not even the beginning of the end. But it is, perhaps, the end of the beginning." My insights about surrendering to God are, at best, the end of the beginning of my learning process.

To show you my level of spiritual perception and devotion in the car that night: I ignored the Holy Spirit's message to me. I continued life and ministry on my terms, as if the conversation with God had never taken place. In the months that followed, however, the Lord often reminded me of His whisper so I would understand He was calling me to give Him more of myself.

During those years as a traveling evangelist, Haley and I had two sons, Cadyn and Gavyn, and God showed favor to our ministry. Our calendar was full with large events and mega-churches. But the commitment God had made in the car on the way to Clinton to teach me about surrender got suddenly serious on one of my more splendid evangelism trips to New York City.

I had been invited to minister in the Big Apple by one of the largest Korean churches in the city. My hosts reserved a room for Haley, the kids, and me at the pricey, plush Crown Plaza Hotel. The church even appointed a chauffeur to show us the sights. This farm kid thought he had arrived! I said to myself, "I could do this kind of ministry the rest of my life!"

Wrong idea.

On the way to the Statue of Liberty, my cell phone rang. (Beware when that happens.) It was a pastor friend from a church in Pine Bluff, Arkansas. He explained that he was resigning to take a church in Memphis and had asked each of his five elders to give him the name of one person they would recommend to be the church's next pastor. He brought a name to their meeting, too, and told me succinctly the results: "Bryan, when we met, all six of us had written the same name—yours." My friend paused for a moment, then pointed out the obvious: "I think this is a sign from God."

In my continuing less-than-fully-surrendered mode, I chose not to arrive at the same conclusion. After all, I had become a big shot (even without having to become a doctor!), speaking at one of the most prestigious churches in the country, riding around in a chauffeured car. I was on top of the world. Why would I leave all this (and the promise of even better to come) to pastor a church in the backwoods of Arkansas? It was ludicrous. And besides, I was an evangelist, not a pastor. Being the shepherd of God's flock,

I rationalized, requires very different talents and passions than I'd ever shown before. I liked blowing in, blowing up, and blowing out of town. Even if I wanted to be a pastor, I wasn't sure I could do it. There were more than enough reasons to say "no." Since the pastor and I were good friends, I could talk honestly with him—and I did.

"I can't see this happening, but I'll pray about it for three days." To which I added glibly, "and then I'll call and tell you I'm not coming."

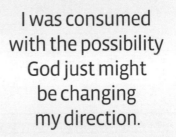

I was consumed with the possibility God just might be changing my direction.

He didn't seem offended by my brush-off, but as soon as I hung up, I had butterflies in my stomach so big they felt like helicopters. Although I have photographs to prove that I went to the Statue of Liberty, I don't remember a minute of it. I was consumed with the possibility God just might be changing my direction.

I'd preached a revival at the church in Pine Bluff and loved the people there, but the town is a little different from most. When I drove in for the revival, I hadn't seen a sign that said "One of the Best 100 Places to Live in the U.S." Instead, the notice at the city limits warned, "Beware of hitchhikers. Prisons nearby." In fact, there are six prisons in the Pine Bluff area.

To make things even less attractive, the city has another major industry: paper mills. If you don't know what a paper mill smells like, I invite you to drive downwind of one for a few minutes and inhale. You'll never forget it! And one more thing: after September 11, 2001, it became known that the second largest stockpile of chemical weapons in the country was located just outside of Pine Bluff. Although it has since been dismantled, back then, if you found an odd box or canister on the side of the road, anyone with sense would leave it completely alone. It might not contain a pleasant surprise. So my idea of Pine Bluff was: wonderful people, but prisons, pulp, and poison—not an attractive combination to lure a young family.

The night after the call from Arkansas, I didn't sleep a wink, even in my elegant Crown Plaza bed. I tossed, turned, and moaned under the burden of an unwanted tug from God.

> The night after the call from Arkansas, I didn't sleep a wink.

Finally, Haley smiled sweetly and said, "Bryan, you're bothering the kids, and I can't sleep either. I know you and God are up to something, but would you mind taking your prayer somewhere else?"

I got up and shuffled to the bathroom where I lay on the floor wrestling with God about my future. As I prayed, cried, and poured out my heart to the Lord, the Spirit showed me that, while I thought I was on the pinnacle, God really had me under a pot. I believed my future was too bright and full of potential to go to Pine Bluff as a pastor, and in fact, some respected leaders even told me later it would be the end of me if I went there. But God wanted me to go because He was planning to use the amazing people and that unique city to transform me into the man God wanted me to be. His leading became insufferable in those three days.

I surrendered and moved our family to Arkansas.

Downward Mobility

Author and psychologist Larry Crabb observes that the poison of "demandingness" is deeply rooted in the hearts of

14

almost every person on the planet.[2] If we've done anything for God—even giving up a wretched sin and found freedom in His forgiveness—we conclude that He now owes us. We long to be on top, to be admired, to have the trappings of wealth so people will notice us.

This description of the human condition isn't about mafia crime bosses. It's about me—and perhaps you. As I wrestled with the Lord by the commode at the Crown Plaza Hotel, God showed me that my heart had become enamored with His gifts of prestige and possessions, so much so that they had crowded out the Giver. I had come to the conclusion that I deserve all this stuff. My demands were ruining my relationships, stealing my heart, and poisoning my walk with God—and I didn't even know it.

One of the lessons of surrender God has to keep teaching me (and unless I miss my guess, He has to continue teaching all of us) is what Pastor Bill Hybels calls the principle of downward mobility[3]. We're in good company. The disciples had been with Jesus almost every day for over three years, but on the night he washed their feet and explained (*again!*) that He was going to pay the price to ransom them, they were too self-absorbed to understand. At the moment of His greatest sacrifice, they argued about who would be the greatest in His kingdom!

Whether or not Jesus rolled His eyes, we don't know. Luke only records the conversation. In response to their ladder climbing, Jesus explains that in His kingdom, things are turned upside down:

> *Instead, the greatest among you should be like the youngest, and the one who rules like the one who serves. For who is greater, the one who*

---

2. Larry Crabb, *Inside Out* (Colorado Springs: Navpress, 2007), 143-166.
3. Bill Hybels, *Descending into Greatness* (Grand Rapids: Zondervan, 1994), 17.

is at the table or the one who serves? Is it not the one who is at the table? But I am among you as one who serves. (Luke 22:26-27)

Among other things, when Jesus said, "Follow me," He meant we should follow His example of humility and service. If He, the Creator and Ruler of the universe, would step out of heaven to become a man and die a horrible death to honor His Father and bring others into the kingdom, why should we think surrender wouldn't be required of us?

> Jesus taught humility, and He modeled it powerfully and persistently.

Over and over, Jesus taught humility, and He modeled it powerfully and persistently. The King of Glory was born in a stable. In the kingdom of God, the last shall be first, up is down, to live we have to die, and the outcasts are welcomed in. We rise only when we bow to worship and stoop to serve. Jesus' display of character wasn't in titles but in towels.

The rewards of obedience, however, were never lost on Jesus. He made sure His followers understood they would experience honor for their humble service. In the conversation when He corrected the disciples' lust for greatness, He reminded them:

You are those who have stood by me in my trials. And I confer on you a kingdom, just as my Father conferred one on me, so that you may eat and drink at my table in my kingdom and sit on thrones, judging the twelve tribes of Israel. (Luke 22:28-30)

The rewards of humility are immense, but they are seldom immediate. And the lessons don't necessarily come easily—as I would soon learn.

Think Outside the Box

1. *Why are you reading this book? What do you hope to get from it?*
2. *How would you define or describe "extravagant devotion"?*
3. *Have there been moments in your life when your worship, devotion, decisions, or surrender could be described as extravagant?*
4. *Who is someone that reflects in his or her own way the kind of extravagance modeled by David and Solomon? How does this person's love for Christ inspire you—or scare you?*
5. *Have you ever received a call—literal or figurative—from God that you wish you hadn't? How did you respond? Is there a call like that coming in to you right now that you need to acknowledge?*
6. *Is there anything about the Pine Bluff story that inspires you? Repulses you?*
7. *How do you react to the idea of "downward mobility" in your life?*

c h a p t e r

bittersweet surrender

We will never come to a point of surrender—and we certainly won't continue to surrender—unless we develop the heartfelt conviction that God is supremely trustworthy. We don't have to have all our questions answered, but we must at least be confident that He has the answers.

To help us get there, we see in the Bible a repeated pattern of godly spiritual life: command, obedience, and miracle. When Jesus stepped up to the tomb of His newly deceased friend Lazarus, He could have moved the stone with no assistance, but He commanded the people there to roll the stone away. He gave them "the dignity of causality" by letting them participate in His miraculous work.

At another point, Jesus asked His followers to pray God would provide workers for the harvest. Almost immediately, He told them, "You are the answer to your own prayers," as He sent them out to preach the gospel and heal the sick. Jesus told the man with the withered hand to stretch it out, and then, when he obeyed, Jesus healed him. He told the crippled man next to the pool to pick up his mat, and he was healed. In the Old Testament, in the New Testament, and still today, God gives commands to His people. When we find the courage to surrender our wills to His in an act of obedience, the Spirit is let loose to work miracles.

Even when things appear to be hopeless, God uses this template of spiritual vitality. Jairus, the synagogue ruler, came to ask Jesus to heal his little girl who was on the verge of death. On the way to the man's house, Jesus stopped to cure a woman of a chronic disease. While He was talking with her, some friends brought news to Jairus that his daughter had died. End of story? Not quite. Jesus looked at the heartbroken father and said, "Don't be afraid; just believe, and she will be healed" (Luke 8:50). In that pivotal moment, Jairus could have thought, "You had your chance to take care of my daughter, but you blew it! I'm done with you." But even in the face of death, Jairus obeyed, trusted, and escorted Jesus to his house. It wasn't hard for the Lord of life to raise a dead girl, but it never would have happened if her father hadn't obeyed the command to trust Jesus.

> God asks us to obey and do the natural thing so He can do the supernatural thing.

God asks us to obey and do the natural thing so He can do the supernatural thing. We can't raise Lazarus or a sick girl from the dead, but we can roll away a stone and take a walk. We can't multiply loaves and fishes, but we can carry baskets. We can't heal the sick, make the lame walk, and give sight to the blind, but we can pray. We can't redeem anyone from sin and hell, but we can open our mouths and share the gospel message.

The problem is that we keep trying to do what only God can do, and we forget our part in the process. We may say we're trusting God with a burden, but too often we're just worrying. We carry our concern to the altar like it's a sack of potatoes, and we tell God, "It's all yours. You take it and work a miracle, Lord." But when we get up, we put the sack over our shoulders, take it home with us, and our anxiety multiplies. God won't work the miracle because we won't let go of the problem. If He were to work supernaturally before we trust Him with our need, we'd somehow think it was our doing, and we would become arrogant. But God is immensely patient. He'll wait until we are humble enough to trust Him to do what only He can do and identify our small part in the process.

Years ago, German theologian Reinhold Niebuhr wrote a prayer that helps clarify the difference between our role and God's:

> *God grant me the serenity*
> *to accept the things I cannot change;*
> *courage to change the things I can;*
> *and wisdom to know the difference.*[4]

Certainly, God's commands sometimes seem odd. When Jesus asked the men to roll the stone away from the tomb, Lazarus' sisters voiced the objections of many in the crowd: "He's been in there four days, and, in case you don't know what happens after that long, he's going to stink!"

At that moment, the men had a choice: to obey and roll the stone away or to shake their heads and walk off because Jesus' command didn't make sense. They chose to obey, and they became participants in one of the most noted miracles in Scripture. If we'll do what only we can do, then God will do what only He can do. If we'll do the possible, God will perform the impossible. If we'll do the natural thing, God will move heaven and earth to do the supernatural thing. He's that extravagant.

The Trapeze

I believe God in His grace gives us moments of choice, to remain stuck in our usual, natural ways or to step out and risk trusting Him. Christian psychiatrist Paul Tournier said

---

4.   Reinhold Niebuhr, edited by Robert McAfee Brown, *The Essential Reinhold Niebuhr: Selected Essays and Addresses* (Yale University Press; New Ed edition (September 10, 1987), 251.

that the most important choices in life are like a trapeze. We hold on to one trapeze bar as we swing in the air. We see the other one near us, but to grab it, we have to let go of the one we're holding. We can think about it for days, weeks, or even years. We can plan the release and grab in our minds until we believe we've covered every angle, but we simply can't grab the new one until we let go of the one we're holding and reach out in faith.

> A life of extravagance means taking action to trust God even when we're afraid.

This concept illustrates what it means to take the risks of extravagant faith. We are holding on to the trapeze bar of old habits, old expectations, and old values. We see the freedom and purpose that God wants to give us, but we have to take bold action: we have to let go of the old and grab the new. In *The Adventure of Living,* Tournier described the opportunity: "The adventurous life is not one exempt from fear, but on the contrary, one that is lived in full knowledge of fears of all kinds, one in which we go forward in spite of our fears."[5] A life of extravagance means taking action to trust God even when we're afraid. Courage isn't the absence of fear but acting in the face of fear.

Many of us look at a new opportunity God has put in front of us, and we want to grab it, but we also want to cling to our current comforts. We remain suspended in mid-air, longing for a glorious future but too timid to let go of the past. At that moment, we have a choice. We can't hold both bars at the same time. To grab the new one, we simply have to let go of the old one.

22

5. Paul Tournier, *The Adventure of Living* (Harper & Row, 1965), 116.

To me, the choice to let go of the old and reach for the new is the "sweet spot" of faith. My life as a popular evangelist may feel like a magnificent way to serve God—and it may have begun with a significant step of faith. Yet God remains more interested in who I become for Him rather than what I do for Him, so when it's time to stretch me again, a new level of surrender is required. I never feel more spiritually alive than when I face this challenge and find the courage to take a bold step—like making a ridiculous career move to a pastorate in Arkansas. At the moment I say "yes," let go, and grab on, I'm risking it all. I'm at a point of submissive vulnerability. If God doesn't come through, I'm sunk. I may be afraid I'll fail and fall, but I must put my life in the hands of God, and He's pleased with that measure of faith. Some of us avoid this moment of risk and vulnerability like it's a plague, but I find it exhilarating because it makes clear just how real God actually is.

23

As we hang in the air, many of us are paralyzed by indecision. We see the glory of the future in a life of devotion to God, but we're not sure we can make it. Not to decide, though, is to decide. I once heard a story about the young Ronald Reagan. As a boy, he stayed with his aunt one summer, and she took him to a shoemaker for a new pair of shoes. The man measured his feet and showed him several shoe styles.

"Son," he asked, "do you want rounded toes or square toes?"

Reagan replied, "I really don't know," and he and his aunt left the shop.

A few days later at a grocery store, Ronald and his aunt happened to meet the shoemaker. He again asked the boy, "Have you decided which toe-style you'd like?"

He scratched his head and smiled, "No, not really."

To the surprise of the boy and his aunt, the man said simply, "I'll have your shoes ready tomorrow."

When they arrived at his shop the next day, he presented the boy with his new pair of shoes—one with a rounded toe and one with a square toe. Decades later, the shoes sat in the Oval Office at the White House. Many visitors asked about the odd pair of shoes, and the President always explained, "Those shoes taught me a valuable lesson: If you don't make your own decisions, someone else will make them for you. I've never forgotten that."

God will bring every one of us to a time to make a decision, to take another step with Him or not. In the Greek language, there are two types of time: *kairos* and *chronos*. Most of us think of time as what we track on our watches and schedules. That's *chronos,* the sequence of moments in chronological order. The other time, *kairos,* is a moment of opportunity or danger. In Scripture, we read that Christ was born "in the fullness of time," and "at the right time, Christ died for the ungodly." God knows the perfect timing for whatever happens.

> God knows the perfect timing for whatever happens.

At certain moments, our linear, chronological time intersects with a moment of opportunity. When this happens, we need to be ready. Young Ronald Reagan missed the crucial moment of choice and ended up with a mismatched pair of shoes. He's not the only one who's made that mistake. History is littered with examples of people who failed to see the opportunities right in front of them, and they missed their moments. Hindsight makes some of them downright amusing. Let me share a few with you.

- In 1895, Lord Kelvin, the British mathematician, physicist and president of the Royal

Society, stated emphatically, "Heavier than air flying machines are impossible."[6]

- The August 2, 1968 edition of *Business Week* magazine reported, "With over 50 foreign cars already on sale here {in America}, the Japanese auto industry isn't likely to carve out a big slice of the U.S. market for itself."[7]

- In 1943, Thomas Watson, the chairman of IBM, observed, "I think there is a world market for about five computers."[8]

- Ken Olson, the president of Digital Equipment Corporation, said in 1977, "There is no reason for any individual to have a computer in their home."[9]

- In 1962, a Decca Recording executive listened to a record by the Beatles and turned down the opportunity to be their label, saying, "We don't like their sound."[10]

- Even geniuses can miss their moment. In 1880, Thomas Edison invented the phonograph, but he remarked that his invention was "of no commercial value."[11]

- On December 4, 1941, the Secretary of the Navy, Frank Knox, stated, "No matter what happens, the U.S. Navy is not going to be caught napping."[12]

25

6. Paul Tournier, *The Adventure of Living* (Harper & Row, 1965), 116.
7. Scott T. Robertson, World Trade, "Japan Sells Its First Cars in the United States," July 1, 2004.
8. Cited by Stephen Shankland, CNET News.com, December 22, 2006.
9. Cited by various sources, including Wikipedia, en.wikipedia.org/wiki/Ken_Olsen.
10. Cited in "Beatles Biography," http://people.whitman.edu/~beanjj/beatles/bios.html.
11. Cited on various sites, including www.2spare.com/item_50221.aspx.
12. Cited by the U.S. Army at www.usarpac.army.mil/history2/history_dec.asp.

Some of these people lived long enough to know they'd been wrong, but some died with smug (but inaccurate) assurance of their sagacity.

I believe God swings the trapeze bar of opportunity toward us many times in our lives. Sometimes it should be obvious, but we fail to notice. One of the greatest gifts God can give us is perception, the ability to see through the fog of life so we notice opportunities. Our perceptions can be muddled both by our preoccupation with life as we know it and by our propensity to think more about the past than to believe God for the future.

For many of us, our memories are bigger than our dreams. We're always looking in the rearview mirror to see where we've been, but it's very dangerous to drive while looking in the rearview mirror. Individuals, churches, businesses, and countries are often preoccupied with the past instead of looking for opportunities in the future. The past—even a painful past—is certain, so it seems more secure and less threatening. The future is full of danger and risk but also of opportunity and hope.

If we notice the trapeze bar swinging in our direction and find the courage to grab it, we'll see God do amazing things. Through Jeremiah, God told the people:

> *For I know the plans I have for you, plans to prosper you and not to harm you, plans to give you hope and a future. Then you will call upon me and come and pray to me, and I will listen to you. You will seek me and find me when you seek me with all your heart. I will be found by you. (Jeremiah 29:11-14)*

What will you experience if you refuse to grab the new trapeze bar? Stagnation, impotence, and spiritual decline. But what can you expect if you grab the bar of God's preferred future? His blessing, His presence, and the adventure of your life. I know which I prefer. Yet learning the right preference can be as tough as it is exhilarating.

Think Outside the Box

1. *What are some trapeze bars of opportunity you've encountered over the past few years? Which ones have you grabbed? Which ones have you missed? Which ones do you need to grab now?*
2. *How does knowing there are no guarantees affect your willingness to take risks?*
3. *On a scale of 0 (nonexistent) to 10 (to the max), how much courage do you have to taste God's goodness and take risks to trust Him? Explain your answer.*
4. *Is there a decision you need to make right now so, like the image in Ronald Reagan's story, you won't end up with shoes that don't match?*
5. *Have you ever experienced a moment when kairos and chronos seemed to converge? Are you struggling with such a moment right now? Does that excite you or make you nervous?*
6. *Do you tend to think of your own future as full of danger and risk or opportunity and hope?*

provide and conquer

When we exercise courageous faith to boldly and generously give of ourselves, our money, or possessions, God opens the floodgates of heaven to pour out His blessings. I've discovered, though, that this often happens at a point of need, not when we have plenty to spare.

Once I arrived in Pine Bluff, I found out that the contractor for the new church building had skipped town, not paid the subcontractors, and left the church to pay (again) for the work the subs had done. The people in the church were liable for this double payment, and I as the new pastor inherited along with them a large, unfair debt. I was angry at God because I wanted to hire more staff, but we didn't have enough money. I wanted to implement new programs, but our finances wouldn't allow it.

Living No-Paycheck to No-Paycheck

Every day, I complained to God about our problems. I made sure He knew I knew they were all His fault. Even my being stuck in Arkansas was something He had done to me that I hadn't thought was a good idea to begin with. Now He'd made a bad plan worse because of the church's precarious financial situation.

Whining one day as I drove down the highway, I prayed, "Lord, even if I gave up my salary for a year and poured it into the debt of our church, it wouldn't make a dent in what we owe."

(Here's a free, bonus recommendation: Don't suggest ideas for your radical obedience to God that He might construe as an offering. He might take you up on it.)

Within minutes, the Holy Spirit began to stir my heart. I sensed Him telling me, "That's actually not such a crazy idea. I can use just that kind of sacrifice to mold your character, and I can use it to inspire the people in your church to love more and sacrifice more than ever. You'll learn about Jehovah Jireh in a way that most people don't know Me. I'll use the seed of your salary to bless you and inspire others to pay for the debt of the church."

God also assured me, "If you'll take this step, I'll break the mindset of poverty in the people in your area. Many of them feel locked into a life of poverty. When they see *your* sacrifice and *My* blessing, it will break the shackles in their hearts, and they'll be free to love and trust Me."

Paying the debt of the church was only part of God's promise. The even bigger promise was to change the expectations of people in the church so they learned to trust God for big things—for the rest of their lives. At that moment, I realized that my *chronos* and God's *kairos* had merged. I was sure that He had led me to make the leap. The problem was that I wasn't the only one who had to jump.

I went home to tell Haley, and we both laughed at the idea, just like Abraham and Sarah laughed at God when He reminded them He was going to miraculously give them a son (more about Abraham and Sarah in Chapter 12). Months passed, and Haley and I didn't act on God's leading. The idea was never far from my thoughts, though. One night during that time, I explained to God what a wretched idea it was: "God, how can I give up my salary?" I pleaded, "If I can't pay my bills, it'll look bad for our church, and it'll make me look like a fool!" On top of that, I pointed out, we had just bought a new house, and Haley was pregnant with our third child.

Then at a pastors' conference in early May 2003, Haley and I listened to Pastor Dan Betzer—the pastor of a large, missions-minded church—preach about the miraculous provision of God. There may not have been another person in the room who needed to hear his message, but it pierced my soul. When he gave the altar call, I went forward because the Spirit had convicted me that I needed to trust Him to provide, and I needed to obey—without excuses, no matter the cost. I fell to the floor and wept. My heart was broken, but obeying still wasn't easy. Hours later, the custodians had to ask me to get up from the floor and leave because they were ready to turn out the lights and lock the doors. I was still wrestling with God's clear directive.

> I fell to the floor and wept. My heart was broken.

That night, Haley and I sat up and talked. For months we had asked God to give us wisdom, and at the pastors' conference we concluded that His leading was crystal clear. It was no longer a question of *if*, but *when*.

A couple of weeks later, we talked again but this time, about the details of what it would look like to go a year without a salary. We had two sons, and we knew that the child inside Haley was the little girl she had longed for. We were going to name her Addisyn. For months, Haley had been planning to paint the baby's room and buy new pink curtains. Now, she realized there would be none of that. I was concerned about the lack of a back-up plan. We had no savings, no rich relatives, and no Plan B if God didn't come through. The specter of foreclosure and being the laughing-stock of the community haunted my mind.

As we got ready for bed that night, I told her, "Honey, let's start this on January the first next year. That'll give us more than half a year to get ready, sell some assets, and be prepared."

She looked at me with an expression of sweet surrender and said, "Bryan, we can either play around with God for six months and then trust Him, or we can just trust Him."

When a man has a woman like that, he'll charge hell with a squirt gun! Haley's courageous faith put steel in my soul, and I was ready to take the step I'd avoided for so long. Two weeks later, I announced to the church that we weren't going to accept a paycheck for a year.

> It's difficult to make a budget when you begin with zero.

I explained that it wasn't primarily about the dollars the church would save each month. I was convinced that God would use the money to sow faith and generosity throughout our family of faith. It's not about cash; it's about courage, character, and revolutionary leadership. You can't ask people to go where you haven't been.

To make it through the year, Haley and I planned to cut our expenses in every way possible. After we got our last paycheck, we sat at our kitchen table to work on our budget. We quickly realized, though, that it's difficult to make a budget when you begin with zero. During the year, we sold most of our assets to get cash for bills. We canceled our cable service, cell phones, and home phone. She asked the barber to teach her how to cut hair. A lot of things we had thought were necessities were really luxuries, and we could live quite well without them. We were down to the bare bones. Every dime was valuable. Regardless of the budget cuts, though, we were still working with no income. Something—or Someone—would have to give. And He did.

One day, a large delivery truck stopped in front of our house and began backing down our driveway. I didn't say a word, but I looked at Haley and thought, *Woman, we don't have enough money to buy a new dishwasher. Have you lost your mind?*

Later she told me she had been thinking, *Bryan, you're crazy. We can't afford any stupid power tools.*

Neither of us owned up to what we were really thinking, but we both blurted out, "I didn't do it!"

Haley and I stared at each other a moment before she gave the obvious instructions: "Well, you'd better go out there, and tell the driver he's pulling up to the wrong house."

I ran out waving my arms. The driver rolled down his window, and I explained, "Hey, I'm afraid you've got the wrong address. We haven't ordered anything. What address are you looking for?"

He checked his order form, and it showed our address. "Is this the Jarrett residence?"

I was puzzled, but I said, "Well, yeah, it is."

He told me, "Then I have a delivery for you."

I asked, "Uh, what is it?"

"A commercial deep freeze."

"A commercial deep freeze? What am I supposed to do with that?"

He was beginning to get a little perturbed with my questions and barked, "Man, I'm busy. I'll deliver it, and you plug it in. That's all there is to it. Now, where do you want it?"

I helped him get it off the truck and went inside to try to explain the unexplainable to Haley. She asked, "What in the world are we going to do with a commercial deep freeze?"

I answered with a grin, "Just plug it in, honey. Just plug it in."

We were, to say the least, perplexed. There was no name on the delivery form to show who bought the appliance for us, and we didn't even have enough frozen food to fill the freezer in our refrigerator.

The next morning, a lady in our church called. Her husband and brother-in-law were in management positions for Tyson Foods and said they felt led to do something to help our family. The Lord put it on their hearts to provide us with a year's supply of meat. When she told me what they were doing she said, "We were afraid you wouldn't have any place to put it. Do you?"

I was stunned, and then it all made sense. I slowly muttered, "A year's supply of meat. Thank you, Lord!"

Some time later, I found out that the lady who bought the freezer for us had never talked to the people who supplied the meat. God had orchestrated it, and both had obeyed His directions. When God told the lady to buy us a freezer, she replied, "Lord, he may already have a freezer."

But the Lord responded, "Just buy him one. And buy the biggest one you can find."

Both people had to respond to the Spirit's prompting for all this to work, and the timing was impeccable. I don't want to think about what would have happened if the meat had arrived a day or two before the freezer!

Meeting Jehovah Jireh Firsthand

I had grown up hearing stories about God's provision, so I shouldn't have been surprised to see God work in such a stunning way. My grandparents lived through the Great Depression, and they had to trust God to provide food for them. They tell incredible stories of God's provision. The knowledge of Jehovah Jireh (the Old Testament name that means "God will provide") wasn't just a concept to them. They knew God would be faithful to provide because they saw Him do it in miraculous ways. Once, their pantry was completely bare, and after a season of prayer, a box of canned meat fell off the back of a truck that was driving through town. On

34

another occasion after a flood, my grandmother was on a walk, praying for food, when she found a huge buffalo fish stuck in a fence near the river. They trusted God because they had no other alternatives. I believe God delights in men and women who are willing to trust Him, especially when there's no safety net. In fact, the only time most of us really know what it means to trust God is when we've run out of other options.

> The One whose name is "I Will Provide" is still around today.

The One whose name is "I Will Provide" is still around today. He's looking for people who will believe Him enough to give Him an opportunity to reveal Himself in power and love. During my year of no salary, I saw it over and over.

Early in my no-paycheck commitment, several businessmen I didn't know well asked me to meet them at their office. These fellows owned and operated a number of restaurants, and although they didn't attend our church, they had heard my story from others in Pine Bluff.

They explained the reason for our meeting: "Pastor, we want to help your family, so we're giving you this certificate that will allow you and your family to eat for free in our restaurants."

They handed me a sheet of paper they had created on one of their computers. There was, I'm quite sure, not another one like it. It read, "For Pastor Jarrett and his family: unlimited menu items at any of our restaurants." I ate lunch at their Subway almost every day for the rest of the year and often polished it off with a frozen treat from their TCBY. I could have become the new spokesperson for a national ad campaign about the "Jarrett diet"!

From time to time, people in our church would give me a worried look and ask, "Pastor, what's going to happen to you and your family if you're not getting paid?"

It's not like I hadn't thought of that question myself, and I always answered, "I can't tell you *how* God will provide, but I'm confident that He *will* provide. When one of His prophets needed food, God sent ravens to give him something to eat. If necessary, God will send ravens for my family and me, too. I'm sure of it."

> God went beyond providing just the necessities for us.

I guess I'd given this explanation to plenty of people throughout the year, because they got the idea I was looking for ravens. On many Sunday nights when I got home, I emptied the pockets of my suit and found a church tithe envelope containing several crumpled $5 and $10 bills. The writing on the outside suggested that an elderly saint had put it in my pocket. Every time, the envelope was inscribed simply "The Ravens."

God went beyond providing just the necessities for us. Word of my bizarre commitment spread throughout the community. The first week after I had raised money to live on by replacing my truck with a ratty, aging Bronco, I decided to get my "new" old vehicle washed. At least it would be clean to start with.

As I pulled into the car wash, a man I didn't know recognized me. "You're the pastor who isn't taking a salary this year for the sake of your church, aren't you?"

I confessed I was the one, and he made a startling offer. The owner of the car wash and garage, he told me that for the remainder of my salary-less existence, I could get my car washed at his place every week and that he would handle my car maintenance for no charge. Even better, the

man and his family had been churchless for a long while
but became regular attenders at our church as a result of
the relationship we developed over clean cars.

My kids were even blessed, despite the best efforts
of Haley and me to cut our family expenses to nothing. As
much as our participation in the YMCA sports teams meant
to us—I was even a coach for my son's baseball team—we
knew our membership had to go. The day I stopped in to
cancel our membership, the manager of the Y became
"suspicious" of my reasons for dropping out. After finding
out our story, he provided a full scholarship for the family's membership so we would stay involved. Later, through
connections I still don't completely grasp, a professional
baseball player on a regional farm team also heard about us.
He sent money to our local YMCA to buy all new equipment
for my son— glove, helmet, bat, ball—and to reimburse the
organization for our family scholarship!

It was also the year I gave my wife the most extravagant gift of our married lives. Christmas happened upon us
about six months into my year of no salary, and about all I
thought I could afford for Haley was a scented candle from
the local gift and jewelry store. I was feeling pretty good
about my thrifty purchase when a jeweler friend, whose
family owned the store, hailed me down.

"Is that all a big church pastor is giving his wife for
Christmas?" he chided, beckoning me into the jewelry
section.

"It will have to do for this year," I offered.

He sensed something serious and toned down his ap-
proach. "Is everything all right?"

Since this guy was a long-time acquaintance, I knew I'd
have to shoot straight with him. Although he didn't know
of my commitment that year, he did know some "deep
background" about my jewelry aspirations. I had talked
with him from time to time about my plan to someday buy

Haley a bona fide wedding ring. At the time we had married, a high-end jewelry purchase was out of the question, and now, ten years into our marriage, my friend thought it was about time to make good on my plans for an upgrade. So to squelch his expectations, I explained my no-salary situation.

Although he seemed to understand the impossibility of my making a major purchase, my friend invited me to join him for a lesson on how to pick out a diamond in case the time came when I could buy one. It sounded interesting, so I followed him through his store to the "diamond room." He laid before me a stunning array of brilliant stones which he said ranged in value from about $1,000 to $40,000. After explaining how to evaluate the differences in size and refinement, he asked which I thought would suit Haley best. I pointed to a cut stone approximately in the middle of the row on the table. Then he had me select a ring to go with it.

"The retail price of your selection," he began, "would probably be a bit over $15,000. My cost, though, is roughly $7,700, and I want to make you an offer. If you'll buy this ring today, I'll charge you only my cost, and you can pay as little as you want for as long as you need to. You can pay $10 a month until Jesus returns if that suits you."

I just stared at him. "I can't. I won't." No matter how low the payments, it would be a debt, and worse, it would look odd (to say the least) if Haley suddenly sprouted a lavish ring while we were penniless.

He pushed me to reconsider and finally insisted on leaving the offer open for 24 hours if I would come back tomorrow to talk with him again. Seeing a way out of a tough negotiation, I agreed.

The next day, I wasn't as prepared for the encounter as I thought I was. The jewelry man had prepared a purchase contract stating the terms he had outlined the day before.

Suddenly, it looked like a once-in-a-lifetime opportunity. People were sure to wonder how the salary-less pastor could manage a ring worth thousands for his wife's Christmas present, but I signed the contract, not quite sure how I would explain myself.

My friend congratulated me on the purchase, then turned abruptly and carried the autographed document to his mother and overseer at the back of the store. She took the contract from him and approached me.

> God became a whole new kind of Jehovah Jireh to me.

"You've made a very fine purchase," she stated matter-of-factly. "And it's important you realize that you now owe us $7,700. Because you just bought this beautiful ring for your wife in spite of your circumstances, it will be an especially meaningful gift to her."

With that, the woman behind the jewelry counter held up the sales contract and ripped it down the middle. "However, it is our privilege to forgive this debt and hope you and your wife enjoy her new ring."

As stunning as the ring "purchase" was for me, it was not the most astounding gift I received during the year of no salary. The most amazing provision was also the most humbling. The news of my no-paycheck year had reached a struggling missionary in Albania who was so encouraged to hear word of God at work in America that he cobbled together funds to send me a check for $100. It might as well have been the widow putting her offering into the temple treasury.

From June 2003 to July 2004 God became a whole new kind of Jehovah Jireh to me. I had reluctantly—and slowly—responded to God's direction to give what to me was a super sacrifice. Yet He showered my family, our church, and

39

me with tangible and intangible blessings. I knew I'd never be the same. I also knew that the joy of living in the sweet spot of my faith was a place I wanted to go back to again and again.

"The rest of the story" was amazing as well: Within eleven months, the debt of the church was paid off. People in our church gave sacrificially. Even *other churches* gave generously to help us.

My original commitment was to go without a salary for a year or until the debt was paid, whichever came first. Since the debt was paid off in eleven months, people asked, "Pastor, are you going to take a salary now?"

I thought and prayed, and the Lord reminded me of the story of the feeding of the 5,000. After everyone was fed, the disciples picked up 12 baskets of leftovers. So I decided, "I'm not going to take a salary for these next four weeks. Let's see how God wants to use the 'leftovers' from all the giving." He had quite a bit of leftovers in mind.

For a long time, the church had been looking for additional land for our school, but no parcel large enough at a price we could manage presented itself. Yet during the leftover period, God led us to a remarkable 28-acre tract of land exactly suited to our needs. With a school building already in place, the property was worth several million dollars, yet our church bought it for just the cost of paying off the owner's debt of $75,000! We saw this as another example of God's blessing for our obedience.

During the whole year, God had provided for Haley, me, and our kids so that we never missed a meal, and we never missed a payment. We had gone without a lot of things—and had nothing left in the bank—but God had provided for every need. It was exhilarating to see God come through for us again and again. In a way, I hated to see it end. We had been living in God's supernatural supply, and when we began receiving paychecks again, we wondered if we were somehow turning off the faucet of God's blessings in our lives. I couldn't wait to live in the sweet spot of risk and blessing again.

Think Outside the Box

1. *Have you ever experienced Jehovah Jireh firsthand through a time when you were radically obedient, showing extravagant devotion to God, and He provided for you in a miraculous way? If so, describe what happened. If not, what does the lack of this experience tell you about your spiritual life?*
2. *Have you ever laughed at a particular thought of doing something crazy for God?*
3. *What feelings did you have as you read the story about going for a year with no salary?*
4. *Consider the story about Haley's ring in light of the scripture that says God will do more than we can ask or think (Ephesians 3:20). Have you ever experienced more from God than you imagined possible?*
5. *Pour out your heart to the Lord about what you've read in this chapter. Tell Him honestly about your hopes and fears, your anger, and your love for Him. Then listen to His Spirit speak to you.*

extravagant is as extravagant does

A life of extravagant devotion to God isn't easy. American Christians swim in a cultural ocean of soul-killing materialism. In the past few years, I've traveled the world preaching the gospel and encouraging believers, but to be honest, I've learned far more from the people in Third World countries than I've taught them. They have far fewer of the material things we enjoy in America, but they have a deeper commitment to God and a higher level of genuine praise than I see in most of our churches. They exhibit "glad surrender" to God and His calling, and God delights in blessing them.

Dream Shift

In our churches, many of us have confused the American Dream with God's call to radical devotion. For this reason, our faith is anorexic—starved and weak. I believe Jesus died to give us much more than we're settling for. He came to bring us life, but we're so distracted by success, pleasure, and approval that we miss Him and His presence, power, and provision. The leaders of the Right Now Campaign (a ministry to help 20- and 30-somethings find opportunities to serve God) have coined a useful term. They say Christians today need to become "traders." Their mission is to help people trade in the pursuit of the American Dream for the pursuit of Christ and the life He wants us to live.

The apostle Paul encourages us to resist letting the world's pressures, values, and distractions squeeze us into its mold. He wrote to the believers in Rome:

Therefore, I urge you, brothers, in view of God's mercy, to offer your bodies as living sacrifices, holy and pleasing to God—this is your spiritual act of worship. Do not conform any longer to the pattern of this world, but be transformed by the renewing of your mind. Then you will be able to test and approve what God's will is—his good, pleasing and perfect will. (Romans 12:1-2)

Notice that Paul doesn't give us a list of things to quit doing to prove we're good Christians. He invites us to think, reflect, and consider the incomparable mercy of God displayed by the death of Jesus on the cross. His sacrifice convinces us that He loves us, and we can trust Him to lead. In response to His love, forgiveness, and power, we enthusiastically say "Yes!" to Him every moment of the day. A life of devotion is a powerful, compelling "yes," not a sour list of "no's."

When our hearts are flooded with the grace of God, we gladly reject things that get in the way of our desire to honor Him. And suddenly—or sometimes gradually—God turns everything upside down in our lives. The paradox of the Christian life is that we win by losing, we receive by giving, the way up is down, we save our lives by losing them, and the way to get power is by giving it all away.

Too often, we are slaves of things that promise to make our lives fun, easy, and rich, but the cost of living for superficial and transient things is far too high. When we merely *dabble* in the things of God, we become spiritually starved. Jesus came to give us an abundant life and establish a kingdom that's countercultural, one where a responsive prostitute or tax collector wins more honor than a king, and

44

a poor widow's meager gift is worth more than the wealth of nations. This kingdom isn't just a *little* different from the one we live in each day. *It's categorically different in every way.* The invitation to follow Jesus is a summons to a revolution—nothing less and nothing else.

Change doesn't happen easily, and it doesn't occur by magic. The transformation of a life occurs only when a person is so desperate for change that remaining stuck in the rut of life is no longer an option. Bill Hybels, pastor of Willow Creek Community Church near Chicago, says God needs to birth in us a "holy discontent." I heartily agree. When I look at all the superficiality and distractions in my life and the lives of those around me, I have a gnawing dissatisfaction, coupled with an eager anticipation, of what the church could be if all Christians would respond in faith and obedience to the grace of God.

> A life of devotion is a powerful, compelling "yes," not a sour list of "no's."

My friend and our church's executive pastor, John Cruz, grew up in Latin America. As he listened to me speak on this subject, he remarked, "What you're teaching the church is relatively easy in the Third World because they don't have many alternatives, but you're trying to tell people in a wealthy culture to hold Christ tightly and their affluence loosely. You're helping people be possessed by God, not by the things they think they possess."

Developing Your Vision

Abraham was a wealthy man—in fact, one of the wealthiest of his day. For him, the potential for evil wasn't in his wealth or possessions but in making an idol of the son God had given him. Instead of holding Isaac with an open hand, he clutched him too tightly, putting the boy in the center of his affections. After the moment of supreme surrender to God on Mt. Moriah, however, everything changed. He was still Isaac's dad, yet Abraham no longer clutched the boy so tightly. Isaac was God's gracious gift, never again to be more important than the Giver. At that point, Abraham experienced "the blessedness of possessing nothing."

When we gaze at the beauty and power of Christ, we have to make a choice. If our hearts are hardened, we shrug our shoulders, mouth the songs at church with little emotion, and remain stuck in a lifestyle of superficiality and meaninglessness. Or, like the apostle Peter, we can answer the call of Christ to take a risk, step out of the boat, and see Him do amazing things in us and through us. When God gives us a challenge, we either progress or regress, taking steps forward in faith or backward in cowardice.

In her book, *Dangerous Surrender,* Kay Warren equates our openhearted and openhanded response to Christ to accepting an undeveloped Polaroid picture. (For those who are too young to remember this revolutionary way of taking pictures, a click of the lens began a process in which you watched as a black image gradually—almost magically—developed into the final photograph.) When Jesus holds out his hand and says, "Follow me," He doesn't explain all that this invitation will entail for us. It's as if He's offering us an undeveloped picture, saying, "Do you want a picture of your future?" We can say "yes," not because we know all the details, but because we trust Him to lead us, strengthen us, and bless us—no matter what the picture of our future looks like as it develops.

There are aspects of a relationship with God that can never be experienced until and unless we fully surrender to Him. As long as God is merely one of the things that are important to us, we'll never know the wondrous joy, peace, and power of walking arm in arm with Him. He must be the one thing that is important to us.

Can we trust God if we devote our lives extravagantly to Him? Yes, He's proven that He's supremely trustworthy. He bankrupted heaven to display the magnificence of His love by sending Christ to die for us. We don't have to worry about His compassion or His intentions for us. I can assure you, though, that if you stay safe in the boat of mediocrity, you'll miss out. Life is an adventure for those who find the courage to take a risk, step out and walk on water with Jesus, for

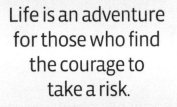

Life is an adventure for those who find the courage to take a risk.

those who trade in the mundane for the extravagant life God offers. As for me and my house, we're committed to being traders.

Think Outside the Box

1. *Do you sense God trying to enlist you in a revolution in the church and in the world? Why or why not?*
2. *How has the American Dream come between you and God?*
3. *Explain in your own words what it means to say that the Kingdom of God is "categorically different in every way" from the usual, worldly way of life.*
4. *Re-read the quote from Romans 12:1-2. In what ways does your mind need to be renewed so you will not be conformed to the world?*
5. *Are you at a point of "dangerous surrender" in your walk with Christ? If so, what step(s) do you need to take?*

living the language of
extravagance

To live a life of extravagant devotion, we need to learn a new language. I call it, not surprisingly, "the language of extravagance."[13] First, we start with a definition that helps us understand the nature of spiritual vitality. *Extravagance* means: "to exceed the appropriate limits of decorum or probability; unrestrained excess." We will only have an extravagant devotion to Christ, however, if we first grasp the extravagance of His incredible gift of grace to us. We don't start with us; we start with Him.

49

Our God is an extravagant God. He "so loved" that "He gave." If we bear His name, we also must exhibit His nature. As our hearts are filled and overflow with wonder and gratitude because Jesus paid the ultimate price to set us free, we'll gladly surrender ourselves to Him and become open channels for His grace to flow from us into the lives of those around us. Our new language may use many terms that are already familiar, but they take on new meaning when we understand them from the viewpoint of the cross. Then, instead of holding back all we can, we give all we can. Instead of wanting to honor ourselves, we want to honor the One who loves us so extravagantly.

---

13.   I am grateful for the teaching of Pastor Robert Morris on the concept of giving and generosity. When I read his book, *The Blessed Life*, I felt inspired to live wholeheartedly for God. He first introduced me to the concept of extravagance, and it then became part of my own language.

The Necessity of a Good Memory

The level of our heartfelt praise and obedience is in direct proportion to our grasp of God's love for us and reflects whether or not we truly live out what we say we believe about the God we serve. Some of us have been Christians so long, sat quietly in so many services, and sung so many songs without riveting our hearts on the Savior that we have forgotten what it was like to be lost. An interviewer once asked Pastor Tim Keller what makes his church so vibrant. Had he found some "key" to church growth? Keller just smiled and explained, "We haven't forgotten what it was like to be lost." The memory keeps their faith strong and their praise fresh.

> Our heartfelt praise and obedience is in direct proportion to our grasp of God's love.

50

When I'm in churches full of recently converted prostitutes, thieves, and drug addicts, there is a power in their worship that can't be beat. The reality of God's grace fills the room because they haven't lost touch with the desperate plight that drove them to the foot of the cross and caused them to cry out for mercy. Novelist and theologian Dorothy Sayers remarked, "None of us feels the true love of God till we realize how wicked we are. But you can't teach people that—they have to learn by experience."[14]

We want to look clean and neat. We want people to think we're good Christians, but when we forget the wickedness in our hearts, we minimize grace, even though grace is our only hope of forgiveness, peace, and glory.

---

14. Dorothy L. Sayers, *The Emperor Constantine, A Chronicle* (Grand Rapids: Eerdmans Publishing Company, 1976).

Addicts, prisoners, and all other self-aware, honest people on the planet are blown away by the fact that a holy God loves them enough to pay the price to free them from sin and adopt them into His family. They sing "Amazing Grace" with wonder in their hearts, shouts of praise on their lips, and tears of thankfulness in their eyes.

The rest of us may look better than these "dregs of society" on the outside, but our hearts are just as wicked as the prisoner on death row. While we may not have committed the same crimes, our self-righteousness stinks in the nostrils of God. When we compare ourselves with others and feel superior, our pride blocks the flow of grace in our lives and makes us modern-day Pharisees. When I'm aware of the selfishness and arrogance in my own heart, I remember again that I'm in desperate need of the Savior's forgiveness. I marvel that the Son of God would step out of the glory in heaven to suffer and die—for me. Because of my sins, I deserve to be where the fire isn't quenched and the worm doesn't die, but God has given me a place at his banquet table with Abraham, Isaac, and Jacob. They, too, were like me, flawed people who reached out to God for forgiveness.

At the end of his life, Paul reflected in one of his letters to Timothy and called himself "the chief of sinners." Paul, the church's strongest leader since Christ, found hope, joy, and strength by remembering his desperate need for forgiveness, not by claiming a false superiority. He really meant what he said about himself. We're the ones that sometimes think of biblical characters as other-worldly heroes.

The Bread, the Cup, and the Mission
Since the first century, Christians have tended to put the twelve disciples so high on a pedestal that we can't imag-

51

ine them as regular, flesh-and-blood people. But they were. In his book, *Twelve Ordinary Men,* author and pastor John MacArthur describes them as "common men, uncommon calling."[15] Christ didn't choose them because they were special, extraordinary, or incredibly gifted. The only extraordinary thing about them was that they were so ordinary: several fishermen, a tax collector, a rebel, and a few others thrown in. They were like the rest of us, unworthy and unqualified. McArthur observes:

> *They were perfectly ordinary men in every way. Not one of them was renowned for scholarship or great erudition. They had no track record as orators or theologians. In fact, they were outsiders as far as the religious establishment of Jesus' day was concerned. They were not outstanding because of any natural talents or intellectual abilities. On the contrary, they were all too prone to mistakes, misstatements, wrong attitudes, lapses of faith, and bitter failure—no one more so than the leader of the group, Peter. Even Jesus remarked that they were slow learners and somewhat spiritually dense (Luke 24:25).[16]*

But Christ saved them, sanctified them, and transformed them into bright lights of His grace to begin a worldwide revolution.

When we feel discouraged because we've concluded that we're "nobodies," we can remember that we're exactly the kind of people Jesus chose to change the world. Actually,

52

---

15. John McArthur, *Twelve Ordinary Men* (Nashville: Thomas Nelson Publishers, 2002), 1.
16. Ibid, xii.

there's not any other kind of person. We're all nobodies until Christ infuses us with His pardon, power, and purpose.

By the time the disciples gathered for the Passover meal with Jesus the night He was betrayed, they had been with Him for about three years. They had seen Him perform miracles and heard Him teach new truth. They had witnessed His tender compassion for hurting people, and they saw His fierce anger at corrupt religious leaders who were leading people away from God. Now, at the Last Supper, Jesus wanted to be sure these men—the ones who were to be entrusted with the enterprise of taking the gospel to the entire world—really "got it." He had talked often about instituting "the kingdom of God" on earth. It wasn't going to be a tidy, exclusive club; it would be a revolution!

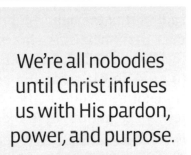

We're all nobodies until Christ infuses us with His pardon, power, and purpose.

When Jesus passed the bread and held up the cup at the Last Supper, He was challenging these men to a radical level of commitment and community that few of us understand. He said the bread was a symbol of His body that would be broken for us. Scripture refers to the church as the Body of Christ. The bread in the Last Supper and the bread in every communion or Eucharist is a symbol of our connection to each other: our community, our togetherness, and our inseparable bond.

Soldiers tell me that the bond they share with men in the same company—and especially in the same foxhole—is the strongest relational connection they know. When people are committed to die for the same cause, the sense of community they share is supernatural. When Jesus said, "Take the bread," He was teaching the disciples—and us—

about true Christian community. Together, we live and die for a shared cause: the honor of our Savior and the extension of His kingdom. This is what it means to be a "missional community."

If the bread symbolizes community, the cup signifies commitment. The wine was a symbol of the blood He would sacrificially spill the next day for them and for us. When He said, "drink the cup," He invited them to let His sacrificial death for their sins sink into the deepest parts of their lives. Nothing hidden. Nothing held back. He wanted them to drink in His grace and power. Only then would they be transformed from the inside out and experience a radical level of commitment to the work of God. Make no mistake: Jesus was inviting them to join Him on the greatest adventure the world has ever known—one that would lead to His death and eventually theirs. He was inviting them to give their lives figuratively and literally. When they put the bread in their mouths and the cup to their lips, they signed a solemn covenant with God and each other.

The cup Jesus blessed and passed around that night was a sign of commitment. As it was passed to each of them, they instinctively understood that their sip of wine was the bold proclamation, "Lord, I'm all in! I'm pushing all the chips to the center of the table. You have all of me."

They drank the cup that night, and they meant it— at least, eleven of them did. Yes, they ran from trouble a couple of hours later, and they hid from the authorities in the weeks after Jesus came out of the tomb. But on the day of Pentecost when the Holy Spirit came upon them in power, they became lions of the faith. In the coming years, they roared with the message of Christ to every corner of the known world. The extravagance of their devotion is seen in their deaths:

54

- Simon the Zealot was crucified, like Jesus, with nails in his hands and feet;
- Jude, also known as Thaddeus, died on a cross;
- Matthew was slain with a pickaxe at Ethopus;
- Philip was scourged, imprisoned, and later stoned to death;
- James the Great was beheaded;
- Thomas was murdered by an enraged, idolatrous priest and rammed through with a spear somewhere in India;
- John was boiled in a pot of hot oil, somehow survived, and was exiled to the island of Patmos off the coast of Turkey;
- Simon Peter was condemned to death by Nero and crucified upside down;
- Andrew was crucified on an X-shaped cross;
- James the Lesser was stoned, and then beaten to death with a fuller's club (a hammer used to groove iron);
- Bartholomew, also known as Nathanael, was filleted alive and then crucified with his head facing downward.[17]

Judas betrayed the Lord that night, and a few hours later, he hanged himself in shame. For Judas, following Jesus was never about selfless devotion or commitment. He was only with Jesus when Jesus had something Judas wanted. Yet Judas wasn't much different from many "consumer" Christians today. When it began to look like following Jesus would cost Judas something, he changed course and scrounged a way to profit from his relationship with Jesus.

---

17. Adapted from John Foxe, *Foxe's Book of Martyrs* (CreateSpace, 2010).

In some types of work, people face a moment of truth when they choose to play it safe or cross a line of reckless abandonment. A policeman finishes training and is assigned to his first duty. A soldier completes boot camp and accepts a combat role. A businessman holds his pen over a contract and decides to sign or not. Drinking the cup was that kind of moment for the original twelve disciples.

> The cross calls us to devote our lives to the One who bought our freedom.

Too often in the American church, we believe the doctrines of the cross, and we can explain the concepts of justification and reconciliation. We know the language, but we don't grasp the implication of these truths. The cross of Christ sets us free from sin, but it calls us to devote every ounce of our lives to the One who bought our freedom. We are, as Paul explained, "no longer our own. We've been bought with a price" (1 Corinthians 6:19-20). Jesus isn't our Sunday Civic Club president, and church shouldn't be just a social gathering. The church is a combination hospital and command center, the place where hurting people receive comfort and the launching pad to conquer and transform the world!

If you grasp this, you'll realize that the purpose of your life doesn't come from having one more possession, one more promotion, or one more pleasure. It comes from knowing that your life really counts in God's kingdom. In his classic book, *The Call*, Os Guinness defines our spiritual calling as:

> *the truth that God calls us to himself so decisively that everything we are, everything we do, and everything we have is invested with a*

special devotion and dynamism lived out as a response to his summons and service."[18]

All of us—not just pastors, church leaders, or overly religious people—have been called to be extravagantly devoted to Jesus, in every way and every day.

Have you taken the bread from Jesus' hand and eaten it? Have you received the cup from Him and taken a long swallow of His grace? If you have, do you really get it? Do you understand that you have contractually surrendered your life to God? If you haven't, the message of this book won't make any sense at all to you—but it can begin to make sense right now. And if the thrill of walking with Jesus has become a distant memory, it's time to dig deep into the recesses of your heart, clear away the cobwebs of complacency, and experience the cleansing flood of His forgiveness in a fresh way. Maybe you've been playing it safe in your relationship with Jesus. It's time to push all your chips to the center of the table and tell Him again—or maybe for the first time—"I'm all in! I surrender. I'm all Yours. I belong to You."

Faith in God isn't just for spectators, and it's not an individual sport. Each of us is part of the Body of Christ, and we all play a vital role in the health of each member and the ability of the Body to accomplish its goals. By taking the bread that night two millennia ago, the men sitting around Jesus were not just committing themselves to God. They were committing themselves to each other. Our relationships are a vital part of the revolution. Jesus challenged His men to join and lead a *coup d'état* to overthrow the status quo—not the Roman government but the normal human condition of self-absorbed living. If they'd drink the

57

---

18.   Os Guinness, *The Call* (Nashville: Word Publishing, 1998), 4.

cup and proclaim their total, unmitigated loyalty to Him, He promised to use them to change the world.

At our church, we explain that people can *belong* before they believe. Those who join us don't have to think like us, act like us, or believe like us to be loved by us. We're convinced that if people will hang around long enough, eventually they'll want to cross the line and move from belonging to believing. Surrender may not happen the first time they walk through our doors, but if they stay long enough and if they open their hearts to the Lord's grace and power, eventually they'll gladly give everything they've got to Jesus.

> All of us are invited to a life of selfless surrender and supernatural empowerment.

58

Some people might read this chapter, examine their hearts, and conclude, "I'm just not there. I don't have that kind of desire to know and follow Christ. This language of commitment isn't for me."

Fair enough, but consider a few questions: Do you *want* to know Jesus like this? Do you long to truly experience His love and power? Is there at least a flicker of interest?

All of us are invited to live a life of selfless surrender and supernatural empowerment, but sadly, few genuinely experience such an extravagant devotion to Jesus. The German theologian and mystic Meister Eckhart identified the starting point for many of us. He wrote, "The soul must long for God in order to be set aflame by God's love; but if the soul cannot yet feel this longing, then it must long for the longing. To long for the longing is also from God."[19] To get there, we must want God like a starving man wants food.

Think Outside the Box

1. *Has anyone ever done something extravagant for you? How did it make you feel? What was your response?*
2. *Define "extravagance" in your own words.*
3. *How did reading the list of ways the various disciples were martyred affect you? Did you find it shocking? Depressing? Inspiring? Challenging?*
4. *How do you need to change your language so as to apply the principles in this chapter?*
5. *What are some specific ways you can communicate with God using the language of extravagance?*
6. *Is faith for you a spectator sport, or are you "on the field"?*

---

19. Quoted by Philip Yancey in *Reaching for the Invisible God* (Grand Rapids: Zondervan, 2004), 208.

chapter 6

hungering for God

After the miracles I experienced during my year without a salary, you might think I was full enough of God's graciousness for a lifetime, that I'd never again lack a deep sense of His closeness and involvement in my life. You might think that, but you'd be wrong. God did make clear His place in my life as Provider. No one could shake my faith in that reality. The issue was settled in my heart and mind. Yet within a month of wrapping up my no-salary year, I already sensed the need for a next step with the Lord.

In His most famous message, Jesus told the crowd, "Blessed are those who hunger and thirst for righteousness, for they will be filled" (Matthew 5:6). I had followed God faithfully to Arkansas, had been pastoring there for more than a year, had seen Him provide supernaturally for all my family's needs, but Jesus' words about hungering and thirsting for righteousness dominated my thoughts. I was desperately hungry and thirsty to experience Christ's leading for what our church should do next. We'd paid off an onerous debt and secured property for expanding our school. We were on fire with enthusiasm for God's work in our midst. As I talked to my mentors about all God was doing, they told me, "Bryan, you need to harness the enthusiasm and vision and do something great. Build a new building, start a high school, inaugurate a huge program—do something big to capture the momentum!" But I didn't sense God leading the church or me in any of those specific directions. The positive inertia was there, yet I was at a loss to know what to do with it.

In my confusion, I wondered why I hungered so for God's leading but couldn't hear Him. My spiritual state prompted me to consider what I could do to seek the Lord. The thought of spiritual hunger connected in my mind with the thought of physical hunger. Could it be that God would speak to me if I were to seek Him through some significant experience of fasting?

> My fast became a call to solemn assembly for us to pursue God together.

The idea was intimidating. Fasting wasn't my favorite spiritual discipline. For years, I'd fasted a day here or a few days there. On a few occasions, I'd even fasted ten days at a time, but I had also felt that someday God would instruct me to fast for forty days. Although the idea of a long fast was an unhappy prospect, the notion grew on me that the time had come. *Chronos* and *kairos* again. The more I thought about it, the more I had to admit God was calling me to a forty-day fast.

Fast Friends

More than I realized, God had been preparing me for this juncture. I had recently met and become fascinated by Bill Bright, the founder of Campus Crusade for Christ. He was a proponent of fasting, and I learned a lot from him that encouraged me to try a serious fast.

Although I found a monastery where I could hole up for the entire forty days, as I prayed, God showed me this was to be a journey for our whole church, not just for me. He wanted me to remain among our people as I fasted so I could lead them and encourage them to pray and fast, too. I announced my intentions to the church, and I guess after my year of no salary, they knew I was serious. My fast became a call to solemn assembly for us to pursue God together. During those weeks, I kept preaching and leading our congregation day in and day out, but the fasting eventually took a toll on me physically. By the last week of my fast, people could tell at a glance something was different about me, and it wasn't that my face was glowing like Moses coming down from Mt. Sinai. I'd lost more weight than any doctor would have encouraged, down from 200 to 157 pounds.

In the last week of the fast, I was too weak to go to the office each day, and I realized it was time to focus the remaining days on simply making it through this trial. A friend offered me the use of a rustic cabin deep in the Arkansas woods, miles from nowhere. I accepted his offer and headed for the forest retreat as a fitting end to my forty-day journey.

Each day at the cabin, I took communion, dove into my devotions, and prayed. By the 38th day, I had expected a miraculous visitation from God. Surely after such a strenuous exercise in spirituality, I deserved some special consideration. Much of my waning energy began to focus on disappointment. God seemed to be letting me down at my point of serious need. In my naïve faith, I truly thought Gabriel and Michael might appear in the cabin and impart to me the mysteries of the kingdom of God! Or surely the "still, small voice" would make itself known in the quiet of the woods (my stomach had long since given up growling). I strained inwardly to hear God's wisdom about the direction of my life and our church, but I heard and saw nothing—nothing at all. It felt like I had wasted away for nothing. God had abandoned me.

My expectations were not entirely unfounded. I reasoned that as the fast progressed, the experience of God's presence would heighten. After all, at some points during the first 38 days, the presence of God was so real I felt like I could touch Him. Surely the end would be the best time yet. In the last few days, however, the heavens were like sealed steel doors. Instead of having my vision clarified during those weeks, I was more confused than ever.

My definition of a leader is "the one who knows what to do next," yet by my own definition, I wasn't a leader anymore. I'd been asked to speak at a denominational convention, but I didn't have a clue what to say to the pastors. As I fasted, I thought God would give me clarity and power, but I struggled in a cloud of confusion and impotence. I began to question my calling, my worth, and my purpose. I felt like more of a liability than an asset to my church and to the kingdom of God. I even considered the possibility that I should give up my position as pastor of our church!

On the 38th morning as I prayed, I lost it. I had what my Southern friends call "a conniption fit." I shook my fist in God's face and blamed Him for not coming through for me.

You may think you need to drop this book and stand back because you expect a bolt of lightning to obliterate it for my blasphemy, but I have news for you: it's not blasphemous to be honest with God. In fact, my anger with Him that morning put me in good company with a host of men and women who have pursued God with all their hearts. God is much more upset with our apathy than by our honest anger. Throughout the psalms, for example, transparency with God is considered a mark of reverence for Him. As we read these poems and songs, we glimpse the writers pouring out their hearts in despair, grief, confusion, and (thinly veiled) rage. Martin Marty observed that over half of the psalms are "wintry," not sunny, but as the psalmists pour out their hearts, they almost always find renewed hope, insight, and courage to follow God.

The Lord is never offended by our rigorous running after Him. He welcomes our honest expression of emotions as a sign of true faith and a longing to know Him. Sometimes, the most productive thing we can do in our spiritual lives is to find a lonely place and have a yelling match with God. One pastor said he sometimes goes for drives down country roads and screams his objections to God's will and ways. This suggestion seems incredibly irreverent to some, but in truth, it helps clear away a lot of phony spirituality and false humility so we can be truly honest with the Master—and honesty is absolutely essential if we're going to have an extravagant relationship with Him. Are you intimate enough to argue with God? I hope so. Our most intense arguments occur in our most intimate relationships because we are only transparent with those we really trust.

> God is much more upset with our apathy than by our honest anger.

So that morning in the cabin, I had a Davidic moment of honesty with God. I yelled and cried. I complained and felt sorry for myself. After a while, I remembered all God had done for my family, our church, and me in the past year, and a wave of shame overwhelmed me. I felt more broken than I'd ever been before, and suddenly, in the place of anger and blame, I overflowed with a fresh sense of gratitude. I experienced God's forgiveness in the depths of my soul, and I realized He hadn't abandoned me at all. I wept in sorrow and relief. After three hours of rage and repentance, I was so exhausted I laid down and fell sleep.

About two hours into my nap, a faint noise woke me up. I opened my eyes to see a large man standing only a few feet from me! He wore a greasy blue uniform. His hands were stained with grease and oil, and he had a glassy, almost dazed, look in his eyes. I thought he was high on meth and was there to kill me.

Sensing my fright, he raised his hands in front of him and assured me, "Sir, I'm not here to hurt you. I'm sorry for not knocking. I drive a service rig, and this morning I left Mississippi on a long haul. I've been praying on my drive." (You'll never know how relieved I was to hear that he'd been *praying*!) "And I was heading down the highway but felt led to turn down this dirt road. I didn't expect anybody to be here."

> This man had something of significance from God to tell me.

"Three hours ago," he continued, "God gave me specific direction—life and death information for someone in spiritual authority. I called my pastor, but I couldn't find him. I called all the pastors I know, but none of them were available. I realized that the message wasn't for any of them. I wondered if I should stop at every church along the highway, but God led me to drive down here. The message, sir, is like a fire in my soul. I can't rest until I deliver it. When I saw your vehicle at the cabin, I got excited." He paused, and then he asked, "Are you the man?"

I explained, "I'm a pastor of a church about an hour from here, and I'm on a forty-day fast to hear the voice of God."

As soon as I said those words, he started to cry. He spoke gently, "Sir, my name is Dale. Would you let me tell you what God has put on my heart to see if the message is for you?"

There was no doubt in my mind that this man had something of significance from God to tell me. I motioned for Dale to sit down before I remembered there was nowhere for him to sit, so he improvised. In my anger a few hours before, I had turned over the coffee table, but Dale picked it up, set it back in place, and sat on it, facing me. He took both of my hands in his. I could tell his faith was genuine and that God had sent him to me, so I relaxed and prepared to receive God's message.

For the next forty minutes, he never loosened his grip on my hands, and he didn't stop talking. At times, I wondered if Dale was an angel instead of a man. He answered every question I'd asked God over the previous 37 days and shared astounding insights into God's heart and intentions.

"Pastor Bryan," he offered at one point, "you're unhappy in the ministry because you've taken your attention off Jesus and His promises. While you're focused on strategies and effectiveness, your heart is divided and you're missing the point—and *Jesus* is the point. If you'll engage *Him* with as much passion and effort as you've poured into your ministry *for* Him, all those other things will flow out of your relationship with Him."

During the forty days, I'd been preaching every Sunday on pursuing the presence of God, but there had been a void in my own heart. Now I suddenly realized I had fasted because I wanted answers, not because I wanted God.

Dale looked into my eyes and said, "Pastor, if you'll pursue Jesus with everything in you and not get caught up in the peripheral things—that means pursue Him with blinders on—the things you've tried to make happen will come as a direct byproduct of your relationship with Him." Then he quoted Jesus: "But seek first his kingdom and his righteousness, and all these things will be given to you as well" (Matthew 6:33).

The heart is desperately wicked and deceived. I'd preached at our church about the need for a radical, complete commitment to God, and I'd fasted for 38 days to hear the voice of God, but I'd still made God's *answers* to my questions a higher priority than God *Himself*. I'd been blind to my own motives and my heart's desires. It took a dear brother speaking God's message to me in a dusty cabin in the piney woods of southern Arkansas for me to get the picture. He showed me that I needed to spend less passion and effort on the success of my tasks and more on my primary assignment of knowing, loving, and serving Jesus Christ. I had to make sure the secondary things were truly secondary, and the ultimate thing was truly the center of my affections and attention.

> God wants me to plan far less and trust Him far more.

I had been worried about the message I'd speak to our denomination, but Dale said to me, "You've been concerned about your word to the nations, but God doesn't want you to share a new doctrine or a new dogma. Just tell them what you already know."

I realized instantly what he meant: I was to tell the story of redemption in my own life and let the Spirit use it to touch others. It felt like I had just stepped into the apostles' shoes in the book of Acts. The miraculous work of God's Spirit in the New Testament church had just happened to me—and it was extravagant!

Invited to Him

On the day Dale sat on the coffee table and held my hands, God invited me into a new level of extravagant devotion to Him. Suddenly, many passages of Scripture took on new meaning. I realized I'd been "weary and heavy laden" by the worries and responsibilities of making life work, but now I could relax, trust God, and watch Him work more powerfully than ever. As my attention shifted from my responsibility to make things happen to trusting God to work in *His* way and in *His* timing, my heart was freed from the oppressive burden. I found a new depth of worship—pure, unbridled, uncomplicated, and passionate worship.

In Revelation, John gives us a picture of this kind of worship. The Spirit let him glimpse the heavenly realms, and he saw 24 elders fall down before God and sing:

> *You are worthy, our Lord and God,*
> *to receive glory and honor and power,*
> *for you created all things,*
> *and by your will they were created*
> *and have their being. (Revelation 4:11)*

I had sung plenty of worship songs before, but now I understood and meant them more than ever. My devotions no longer focused on what I could learn but on connecting with the Teacher. The invitation to go to a deeper level of devotion gave me more of what really satisfies: true peace, purpose, and power.

Finally, Dale spoke these cryptic words: "Pastor Bryan, make your plans short. Your future has already been decided."

Later, when I told Haley about it, she looked concerned and asked, "Does that mean you're going to die?"

"No," I assured her, "it's an invitation to trust God, to surrender, and to rest. I don't make the plans; He does. I think he means that God has given me an undeveloped Polaroid. Instead of striving so hard to make things happen, God wants me to plan far less and trust Him far more. He's in control. I don't have to orchestrate everything that happens."

Before he left the cabin that day, Dale told me, "God wants you to converse with Him for the rest of your life the way Solomon conversed with God."

The minute he drove away, I grabbed my Bible and began devouring the biblical accounts of Solomon's conver-

69

sations with God. When Solomon became king, he made an extravagant offering that captured God's heart. God was so impressed with the king's display of affection and worship that He offered him anything he wanted. As I explained in Chapter 1, Solomon humbly asked God for wisdom and intimacy. That's what I wanted, too. That's what I had been so desperately longing for—God's presence in my life for the rest of my life.

In *The Pursuit of God,* Tozer describes why we sometimes miss intimacy with our heavenly Father:

> *I want deliberately to encourage this mighty longing after God. The lack of it has brought us to our present low estate. The stiff and wooden quality about our religious lives is a result of our lack of holy desire. Complacency is a deadly foe of all spiritual growth. Acute desire must be present or there will be no manifestation of Christ to His people. He waits to be wanted. Too bad that with many of us He waits so long, so very long, in vain.[20]*

God went to great lengths to shatter my presumptions about His character and His will for my life so He could teach me a new level of extravagant devotion. He wants all of us to have this kind of relationship with Him. In fact, every blessing we enjoy invites us to see Him as ever more beautiful and gracious toward us. Every heartache shows us the depth of our need for Him. What will it take for you to long for Him with all your heart?

70

---

20. Tozer, *The Pursuit of God,* 15.

Think Outside the Box

1. *On a scale of 0 (none) to 10 (totally!), how much do you hunger and thirst for righteousness? What does that tell you?*
2. *Does the idea of fasting intimidate you? Excite you? Do you need to try it?*
3. *Why is it important to acknowledge your heart's wickedness as a precondition for experiencing God's grace? How can you tell if you're really convinced of the heart's depravity?*
4. *What are some lessons I learned from Dale that apply to you? What would these lessons look like if you lived according to them? What are the consequences if you ignore them?*
5. *Who's the main point of your life right now, you or Jesus?*

71

with all your heart

Over and over in the Scriptures, we find instructions and encouragement to put first things first. When Jesus went to the home of Mary and Martha, Mary sat at Jesus' feet to know Him and learn from Him, but Martha became consumed with making a nice dinner for her guests. She resented her sister's choice to "abandon" her to be with Jesus, and she complained to Him about it. Jesus gently corrected her, "Martha, Martha, you are worried and upset about many things, but only one thing is needed. Mary has chosen what is better, and it will not be taken away from her" (Luke 10:41-42).

Paul was well aware of the myriad distractions that threatened to derail the faith of believers in his day in the same way they threaten us. Competing values, multiplied responsibilities, and countless voices can drown out the "still, small voice" of the Spirit. Paul warned the Christians in Corinth, "But I am afraid that just as Eve was deceived by the serpent's cunning, your minds may somehow be led astray from your sincere and pure devotion to Christ" (2 Corinthians 11:3).

Paul was as strong as garlic. He boldly went from city to city to proclaim the gospel, knowing he would be beaten, imprisoned, and flogged. So when he says, "But I am afraid," we need to sit up and take notice. What was this brave man afraid of? He was afraid the Christians would believe the deceptive promises of the evil one, and their pure faith in Christ would be diluted. I believe Paul is saying the same thing to us today. If we're not careful, we'll get too busy, and we'll let the noise around us get so loud that we miss the purity and joy of knowing Jesus.

One Thing

As a husband, father, friend, and pastor, I want to be the best I can be, but through my conversation in the cabin with Dale, it became painfully clear I had become so absorbed in my pursuit of excellence in all these areas, I had taken my eyes off the center of the target: Jesus Himself. I was accomplishing a host of tasks that were on my to-do list each day, but I was failing in the greatest *assignment* God had given me. In a beautiful psalm of surrender, David describes his assignment from God. When we take stock of David's words, we need to remember that he wasn't a monk cloistered away from the stresses of life. He was the king of Israel, daily facing enormous challenges and responsibilities—far greater than I'll ever shoulder. But he understood the essence of the same message Jesus offered Martha and with which Paul warned the Corinthians. Psalm 27:4 describes what our focus should be:

> *One thing I ask of the Lord,*
> *this is what I seek:*
> *that I may dwell in the house of the Lord*
> *all the days of my life,*
> *to gaze upon the beauty of the Lord*
> *and to seek him in his temple.*

"One thing." Not a hundred things, not twenty, and not even two—just one. David's passion, his heart's desire, his aim was to hold God at the unchallenged center of his life. He had crushing responsibilities in leading the kingdom. Whereas most people who lead organizations, businesses, or government agencies get completely absorbed in the duties and the prestige of the job, David didn't let that happen. He riveted his heart on the most important relationship and his highest priority: knowing, loving, and serving God. As he gazed upon God, he found the Lord to be "beautiful."

When a person, a work of art, or a scene in nature is beautiful to us, we delight in it. We can't stop thinking about it and want to tell everyone about its loveliness. Is God that beautiful to you today? Do thoughts of Him delight you, or do they scare you, or worse, bore you? These are questions I have to ask myself from time to time, especially when I sense my heart slipping into duty instead of delighting in the Lord's beauty.

> A heart of dependence on God shows that we have our assignment right.

75

Be a Nothing for Him

Too often, we foolishly cling to the illusion that we can control our situations and the people around us, that we can be the center of the universe. But at some point, we have to face the reality that we are tragically flawed, woefully ignorant, and without the power to change much at all. Thomas Merton once observed, "The reason we never enter into the deepest reality of our relationship with God is that we so seldom acknowledge our utter nothingness before him."[21] Merton's insight is the gateway to sweet surrender.

A heart of dependence on God shows that we have our assignment right. We aren't letting all the tasks of each day, the thousands of nagging responsibilities, and

---

21. Cited by Lisa Harper in *Tough Love, Tender Mercies* (Wheaton: Tyndale House Publishers, 2005), 45.

any misplaced expectations erode our joy like sandpaper wearing away a piece of wood. When we delight in God as our first priority, amazing things happen to us. Scripture provides some eye-opening stories about what can happen for people who focus on God's ability to handle things rather than their own. At a week-long festival in Jerusalem, the sacrifices and ceremonies became more important each day, leading to a crescendo on the final day. Jesus was there, and John tells us in his gospel:

> On the last and greatest day of the Feast, Jesus stood and said in a loud voice, "If anyone is thirsty, let him come to me and drink. Whoever believes in me, as the Scripture has said, streams of living water will flow from within him." By this he meant the Spirit, whom those who believed in him were later to receive. (John 7:37-39)

We have to make choices in walking with God, but when we choose to put Him first, God so desires to pour out His Spirit in us that His love, forgiveness, and power overflow into our homes, our offices, our neighborhoods, and our churches. When we tap into the Source of living water, we experience supernatural empowerment to care about things we didn't care for before, love people we avoided, and act boldly to do God's will. As we yield our hearts to God, we open a channel for His Spirit to flow *into us* to fill us and *out of us* as an overflow of His grace to those around us. Are you experiencing His flow in your life? What is flowing from you right now? Or maybe a better question is: What would your family and friends say is flowing from you?

Character Development
In our culture, we are doers. A person's character isn't as important to many of us as a person's performance. But the

message of Scripture is that character counts. In the famous description of love in his first letter to the Corinthians, Paul says it doesn't matter what spiritual gifts you have or how devoted you are to the cause. If you don't have love, you're just a *Gong Show!* Love, though, can't be manufactured. It must be forged in a transformed heart. The Christian life—a life of surrender to God's love and His will—focuses first on *being* instead of *doing*. Only in *being* God's beloved child will we even *want* to do the things that really please Him.

> Our goal shouldn't be to become known as "nice Christians."

We often define others and ourselves by our doing, but the message of Scripture is that our being, our sense of identity, shapes our actions. Doing flows from who we are. Our goal shouldn't be to become known as "nice Christians" because we show up on Sunday morning, tithe, work in the nursery, or cuss sparingly. Those aren't bad things, but they aren't central things. At best, these things miss the point; at worst, they get in the way of true spirituality.

Too many of us are like the elder brother in Jesus' story of a loving father and his two sons: he was doing right things for wrong reasons. True, the younger son had spurned his father's love and wasted the inheritance given him, but when he returned, he was truly sorry. Although the older brother had stayed home, his attitude revealed that he was merely doing his duty, not honoring his father joyfully by his work. When we're like the older son, his way of living leaves us empty, angry, and confused. We feel self-righteous because we think we've done enough to earn God's blessing, but in truth, we're filled with self-pity because God doesn't jump through our hoops and meet our expectations. When we finally recognize that self-righteousness and self-reliance don't work, we will go back to the heart of the matter, peel back the layers of empty religion, and delight in the beauty of Jesus.

I know this well from the way Christ has worked in my own life. As I mentioned in Chapter 1, I first encountered Him at age seven, but that's barely the beginning of God's work in my life.

> "Life" overwhelmed the Spirit of God in me as a young boy.

I grew up in a devoted Christian family, living with my grandparents. My grandfather was a pastor, and I traveled regularly with him to church, about a twenty-minute ride away. One Sunday night on the way home from my granddad's church, I felt the tug on my heart to follow Christ. Describing the feelings to my grandfather as we rode together, he recognized the seriousness of my desire to know the Lord. At home, he called together all of our nearby relatives to share the joy of my responding to Jesus. That night, he led me in the sinner's prayer to begin a new life in Christ—or so he hoped.

My experience with Christ that night was real, but so were the struggles I faced during my growing up years. Despite my grandparents' love for me and faithfulness to the Lord, "life" overwhelmed the Spirit of God in me as a young boy.

I lived with my grandfather and grandmother because of the serious dysfunction of my parents' marriage. My father left my mother repeatedly, but for years she received him back each time he chose to return. It was during his times away that Mom and I lived with my grandparents.

Even life with my grandparents, though, was difficult. A predatory distant relative began to abuse me sexually during my pre-school years. As is typical with such situations, I was too ashamed to reveal the relative's actions to my mother or grandparents, so it continued whenever my mom and I were living nearby. Finally, at age 12, I recognized the abuse for the evil it was and stood my ground against allowing it to continue. Much emotional and spiritual damage had been done by that time, though, and it took a grievous toll on my inner life.

As genuine as my grandparents were in their walk with God, they followed the holiness tradition which brings with it a rigid adherence to pietistic ways. The anger and pain in my soul joined a disenchantment with church to foster a secret rebellion in my heart. I began to hang out with kids who were older than I, and at age 12, took my first—but far from last—drink of alcohol. Sadly, these friends came from families my mother and grandparents knew and trusted, but they provide a clear example of the problem Paul addresses when he says "bad company ruins good morals." In addition to using alcohol to "fit in" with other kids and to distance myself from a legalistic, religious moral code, I used it to dull the overwhelming pain in my heart.

Ours was a small farm town, and I was an athlete (not an especially good one, but at least I played football—which mattered to people there). I took advantage of the status sports offered: I dated the "right" girls and ran with the "right" crowd. Unfortunately, that "opportunity" put me in the company of people who encouraged the worst in my character and accompanying behavior. I developed stealthy ways to hide my drinking from my mother, and on nights when I planned to get drunk, I made arrangements to spend the night with a friend.

By the time I was 15, I was a bona fide alcoholic, thanks to surprisingly easy access to booze. Older friends were all too willing to buy it for me, and at the time, liquor stores in our area were disturbingly lax in selling alcohol to anyone with the money, regardless of age. Even so, my appetite for drinking eventually outstripped my ability to pay for it. By 16, I was stealing alcohol from the grocery store where I worked. My thefts were so well-refined that no one ever suspected me.

One Fourth of July, my celebration centered around consuming as many varieties of alcohol as I could get my hands on. That night, I was so intoxicated I would have drowned in my own vomit if a friend hadn't turned me over so I could breathe. I vaguely remembered nearly suffocating yet being unable to help myself, and my hangover the next day was the sickest I'd ever been. Realizing how close I'd come to dying frightened me badly. I swore I would stop drinking, but attempting that in my own strength got me nowhere. Within a few days, I was drunk again.

All through these wild but desperate days, I knew what was right the whole time. I was never really a "bad kid." Although my addiction made me devious, I was never mean to anyone, and I certainly never wanted to hurt anybody. No matter how much I drank or partied, I always managed to keep my grades up. I was nice to my teachers and to Mom ("yes, Ma'am/no Ma'am" peppered my vocabulary and enhanced my image for grown-ups). I even made it into the National Honor Society. But despite outward appearances, my 16-year-old life was out of control: I couldn't *not* drink. God knew my predicament, of course, and used an odd turn of geologic events to get my attention.

The Arkansas world of 1990 was literally shaky. Earthquake scientists spent much of that year pinpointing the time at which the New Madrid Fault near the Mississippi River would once again produce one of the most powerful earthquakes on record. It had happened twice before, in the early nineteenth century, and was due to happen again. The date December 3, 1990, had become ground-zero time for the quake. Residents of the area stashed food and water to

80

prepare for calamity, and experts even predicted how many people would die in the massive quake. News of the potential disaster pierced the haze of alcohol and inspired me to think more seriously about eternity and my own mortality than at any time since my more juvenile thoughts at age seven. Although I had never specifically quit believing the truth about eternity, I had put my spirituality "on hold" for later.

About two weeks before the New Madrid fault was due to rupture, my own life quaked. On Saturday night, November 17, 1990, I partied long and hard, and, unlike most such binges, I chose to come home—soused nearly beyond recognition. My timing was bad, and Mom met me at the door. There was no more hiding my lifestyle or the rebellion in my heart. I brushed passed, ignoring her questions about what I'd been doing.

> It broke my heart to hear her pray so desperately for me.

Saturday night was long past. My mother had fixed breakfast and was already getting ready to go to church. Somehow, I managed to eat and then staggered to my bedroom. From my door, Mom asked me to go with her to church. I refused. The next thing I remember is my mother's vocal prayers from the bathroom—her personal "prayer closet." It broke my heart to hear her pray so desperately for me, but she took courage from the Lord and returned to my room with an uncharacteristic holy boldness.

"Get up. You're going to church with me."

"No."

"Yes. You are. You just ate food I cooked and paid for. If you want to eat another meal here, you're going to church with me. This room you sleep in? I pay the bills for it. And if you want to spend another night in this house, go get in the car. The clothes that are on your back, I bought for you. And if you want to wear them again, you're coming with me. If not, be gone when I come home."

Through my stupor, I knew she was serious. I had no time to clean up or change clothes, so I showed up the most ragged, disgusting person at church that morning. I survived the service, and by God's grace returned to church that evening.

In his Sunday night sermon, the pastor proclaimed, "There are some of you here who know it all in your head, but it's made no difference in your heart and in your life. You're like a sponge—a frame with holes in it, waiting to be filled. You've been trying to fill those empty spaces with other things than God, and it's left you deeply lacking." Had he looked into my soul? He was talking about me.

> Only the Holy Spirit can create Christ-likeness in us.

82

"God can satisfy," the pastor continued. "You don't need any more information about Him. You just need to decide. Will you let God fill the holes for you?"

I detested the person I had become and couldn't avoid the truth. At the altar call, I dragged myself to the front of the sanctuary, knowing I must get right with the Lord but terrified I would fail to change. Would I be drunk again by Friday and this last hope gone?

God graciously magnified the mustard-seed faith I offered Him that Sunday night. My faltering steps forward began a twenty-year journey of walking with Him. They also began the true development of my character at the hands of Jesus Christ. We can never construct for ourselves a character that endures the opportunities for evil this life offers. Only the Holy Spirit, given free reign in our hearts, can create Christ-likeness in us.

Two-Way Transformation

The transformation of our hearts happens in two ways: instantly and progressively. The moment we trust in Christ as our Savior, we are delivered from the domain of darkness and transferred into the kingdom of God. We are born again, redeemed by the blood of Christ, forgiven and adopted by God. But our ability to experience this new truth takes time and attention.

Sociologists have identified four stages of development in any undertaking, and they are helpful in understanding the care and discipline required to live a life of faithfulness to Christ. I briefly describe each stage below and point out how I have experienced it in my progress with the Lord.

1. *When we begin a new endeavor, we are unconsciously unskilled. We don't know what we don't know. We make a lot of mistakes, and quite often, we're not even aware that we're making all these blunders. This manifested itself when I was a first-year student in seminary. Too sure of my own abilities, I didn't think I really needed to be in school. After all, I had a vision for ministry and a calling from God. Shouldn't that be enough? As I'm sure my seminary professors could have told you, I had no idea how much I didn't know and still needed to learn.*

2. *Soon, though, I came to the second phase. I realized how much I didn't know (a good thing). Finally, I saw that I wasn't so smart after all. There was a lot I needed to learn, and I became consciously unskilled. Face to face with my ignorance, I became a voracious learner. Humble acceptance of this stage is the key to all future learning.*

3. *In the third stage, a person becomes consciously skilled. Study has had its effect, and the individual's competence grows. Those tasks at which a person was formerly clumsy have become do-able but still with*

83

focus and effort required. I find myself growing in skill but continuing to exert considerable effort to perform well in the craft of leadership, preaching, and teaching. To continue my progress, I analyze everything I do in this third stage of development. I'm in the process of becoming.

4. *In stage four—unconsciously skilled—principles and practices are increasingly ingrained, and the learner no longer has to think about everything he or she does. In my life, the principles and practices of leadership are becoming part of who I am. Rather than focusing on exercising the skills I've acquired, some things are beginning to "come naturally" to me.*[22]

This pattern of progress is true in our spiritual lives as disciples of Christ, but many of us never get beyond the first stage. We think that becoming a Christian is the end, yet it's only the beginning. Progress is possible only by remaining connected to the Source of life.

Some people are as ineffective as a fireman who points his hose at a fire without hooking the other end to the hydrant. His first and most important assignment was to make sure he was connected to the water source. Only then could the water flow for him to fulfill his task of putting out the fire.

Too often, others see only a trickle of living water from Christians, not the flood Jesus promised. And sometimes they see just barren ground with no water at all. It's little wonder non-believers aren't attracted to this kind of dryness. They are made by God to long for extravagant love,

---

22.   These four stages are cited by a number of authors, including Gerard J. Puccio, Mary Murdock, and Marie Mance in *Creative Leadership: Skills That Drive Change* (Thousand Oaks, CA: Sage Publications, 2007), 247-251.

and they're waiting for us to experience it so we can share it with them.

To fulfill your calling as a disciple of Jesus Christ, you must become a passionate learner, internalizing grace and truth so God's ways are no longer just a set of rules to follow. *Doing the right things* isn't complete until the heart of Jesus forms in you, and you become Spirit-filled, Spirit-empowered, and Spirit-led for God. When your identity is transformed through this ongoing development, you can become *unconsciously skilled* as a believer. At that point, you no longer have to try so hard all the time and can simply let the Spirit flow through you.

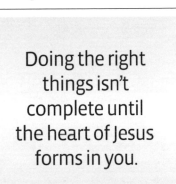

Doing the right things isn't complete until the heart of Jesus forms in you.

85

It's true that, until the day you die, you'll face a struggle between the old nature and the new, but your mind is being renewed as long as you stay connected to God through His Word. Gradually, you'll fight more fiercely and victoriously in the daily struggle to let Christ's love shine and His Spirit flow though you. That's when, like Mary, you've chosen the *one thing* and can follow God with all your heart.

Think Outside the Box

1. *Is there anything in your life that is keeping your eyes off of the "one thing"?*
2. *Where are you in recognizing your "nothingness" before God?*
3. *Are you aware of the character development issues God is working on in your life? If so, what are they? If not, what are you missing?*

4. *Tell someone the testimony of your salvation. If you don't have a testimony to tell, talk to your pastor or a Christian friend about what you need to do to be saved.*
5. *Think of various facets of life—spiritual, relationship, career, parenting, etc.—and evaluate where you are on the spectrum of unconsciously unskilled to unconsciously skilled.*

c h a  t e r

what you give is
what you get

In our progress as followers of Christ, the language of extravagance we talked about in Chapter 5 becomes more comfortable. For the results to bear fruit in us, though, requires the process of a learner.

I've known people who have made a dramatic statement of surrender, such as, "Jesus, I'm all in," and they expected their lives to be full of joy, truth, and glory from that moment on. They didn't understand that there are certain things a Christian must do in order to be an effective disciple. There are specific benchmarks for extravagant devotion, and it's essential to know what they are. Otherwise, it's hard to know what we're supposed to learn and grow in as followers of Jesus. In this chapter, I'll explain four keys to becoming an unconsciously skilled, extravagantly devoted Christ follower: complete trust, uncommon obedience, courageous faith, and outrageous generosity.

Complete Trust

Sometimes I hear people say that trusting in God requires "blind faith." According to Scripture, though, God proves His love and power countless times, in countless ways, to countless people. He doesn't ask us to close our eyes and just hope He's there. He invites us to open our eyes and see all the wonders He has created, the historical reality of the life, death, and resurrection of Jesus, and the way He has worked in and through people for centuries.

When John the Baptist was in prison and doubted that Jesus was the Messiah, Jesus sent back word about the tangible things He had done: heal the sick, raise the dead, give sight to the blind, and preach the gospel everywhere He went. When John doubted, Jesus pointed him to the *facts*.

To communicate a similar message, Luke describes a terrifying event in the lives of the disciples. Jesus is asleep in the boat in which the group is crossing the Sea of Galilee when a vicious storm threatens to sink their vessel. Although they had seen Jesus perform miracles everywhere He went, in this desperate moment, they panic. They rouse Jesus, who calmly stops the raging sea and howling winds. He then turns to the amazed men and asks, "Where is your faith?" (Luke 8:25). The implication of Jesus' question is clear: "You should have known better. Haven't you seen enough of My power and love to trust Me in a storm?" The facts of what Jesus had demonstrated should have been sufficient to sustain the disciples' faith. He had not kept His power a secret, and He expected them to have faith commensurate with the evidence they had witnessed.

Similarly, our faith—our complete trust—is based on the evidence of Christ's power at work as seen in Scripture and in the lives of people around us. The only thing "blind" about our faith is the perspective we sometimes have on the problems that assail us. From time to time, we encounter roadblocks that confuse or infuriate us. We've been following God faithfully, but now we're stuck in our tracks. We feel like shaking our fist at God and saying, "This isn't fair! I thought you were going to come through for me." In those times—and every believer eventually faces such a "dark night of the soul"—we have to cling to God in spite of our perceptions and feelings. We cling to the reality of what we know to be true. We trust Him even in the darkness and hold on to Him even when we don't see the road ahead, just as John the Baptist had to do in prison.

Wonder and gratitude are essential elements for a life of complete trust in God. We can't manufacture this kind of faith out of thin air. Faith is forged in the darkness or in the hot fires of disappointment, and in those critical moments, we look again to the two neon signs of God's greatness and grace: creation and the cross. When we marvel at the sheer size of all God has made, the billions of galaxies, each containing billions of stars, we realize that nothing in our lives is too big for God to handle. And when we gaze upon the cross, the willing sacrifice of Jesus shouts about His tender, insistent love for us. The Scriptures invite us to think, consider, and ponder the greatness and grace of God, and when we do, our faith is infused with praise and thanksgiving.

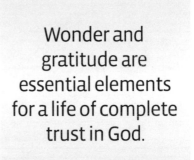

Wonder and gratitude are essential elements for a life of complete trust in God.

89

The invitation to take bold risks, however, isn't just for times when we encounter dark nights and difficulties. It can be an invitation to trust God during a season of blessing, to unlock greater fruitfulness and amazing possibilities of seeing the Spirit work in and through us.

Uncommon Obedience

If you never sense Christ asking you to do something that makes you uncomfortable, it's questionable whether or not you're actually following Him. More than likely, you're just going through the motions of a sanitized, watered-down version of Christianity—the stuff of mere religion.

Jesus calls people to give up the idols of their hearts, to forsake all, and to make Him their first priority. Our old nature wants to make deals with Him, but He'll never settle for that. He demands love and loyalty, and sometimes He tests us to see if we really mean what we say about Him being our *Lord*. The great news is that His tests are a sure sign of belonging to Him.

Scripture clearly describes many of God's requirements. The Ten Commandments call us to a life of love, honesty, and honor. But sometimes, His directives seem to make no sense at all. The Syrian general Naaman discovered this uncomfortable reality. Naaman was one of the greatest military command-

> Obedience sets miracles in motion.

ers of the ancient world. He had led his army to magnificent victories, winning the acclaim of his king and his nation. But Naaman had a problem: he was a leper. He discovered, though, that the solution was right in front of him.

Naaman's troops had captured a girl from Israel in one of their raids, and the general had taken her into his home as a servant. One day, she offered some advice: "If only my master would see the prophet who is in Samaria! He would cure him of his leprosy" (2 Kings 5:3). Desperate, Naaman took the girl's advice. He made plans to go to Israel to see the prophet Elisha, and he packed a fortune in gold, silver, and clothes to pay for his healing. When the Syrian arrived at the prophet's house, however, the dusty man of God didn't even to come to the door to meet the renowned general. Elisha merely sent word by a servant that Naaman should visit the Jordan River and wash there seven times.

Naaman was outraged. The instructions were clear and simple—too matter-of-fact for the magnitude of the general's degrading disease. He felt insulted and didn't think the muddy trickle of the Jordan should offer more healing powers than the mighty rivers of his homeland. Naaman nearly rode away in a huff, but his servants convinced him to give Elisha's remedy a try. Likely with serious mixed emotions, Naaman dipped in the Jordan seven times, and his obedience paid off. God restored his skin, as fresh and clean as a child's.

Throughout the Bible, we find that *obedience sets miracles in motion*. Ten lepers asked Jesus to heal them, and they were completely cleansed of their disease when they obeyed Jesus' instruction and walked toward the priests. Jesus told the blind man to wash in the Pool of Siloam and the lame man to take up his mat. He told the man with a withered hand to stretch out his hand, and he instructed the people at Lazarus' tomb to roll away the stone. In each case (and many others), a simple act of obedience unleashed God's miraculous power.

Until someone finds the courage to take a step to obey, the dam of unbelief and passivity holds the miracle back. As we see more of who God is—more of His incomparable power and love—our motivation to obey changes, and our desire to obey intensifies. With new insights about His character and His purposes, we don't surrender to Him with clenched teeth. We humbly bow and follow His leading because we're convinced He is supremely trustworthy, even when we don't know where He is leading us.

In our day, the concept of obedience has become very unpopular because people see it as infringing on the right to make their own choices. We live in a world of radical self-reliance and self-expression, and we resent anyone—family member, employer, government, pastor, or God—who asks us to sacrifice *at all*. As long as we hold this view, however, we won't be disciples of Jesus. Instead of insisting on our rights, when we grasp the depth of the gospel of grace, we realize we have *nothing* apart from Him! We belong to Him—heart, body, mind, and soul. Instead of resenting His invitations and interpreting His instructions as demands, we look for ways to please Him. Paul described the nature of glad obedience this way:

> For Christ's love compels us, because we are convinced that one died for all, and therefore all died. And he died for all, that those who live should no longer live for themselves but for him who died for them and was raised again (2 Corinthians 5:14-15).

Sweet surrender means that we love Jesus so much we truly want to obey Him.

Courageous Faith

When our hearts belong to Jesus, we're willing to take any risk, give any possession, talk to any person, stand up for any truth, go anywhere, and do anything He wants us to do. It's popular in some Christian circles to focus on prosperity and the promises of God's blessings. While I fully believe in God's desire to bless us, that's only half of the truth. He also leads us into darkness and sacrifice, and if you don't know what I'm talking about, I wonder if you really understand the whole message of the gospel. God not only comforts the afflicted, He also afflicts the comfortable. No one is immune.

Many Christians who have walked with God during tough times recount that their times of deepest intimacy with God and most significant blessings were during or after experiences of suffering and sacrifice. They realized it was precisely those painful times that drove them to the heart of God. That's why He leads people into darkness: so that we'll take His arm and lean on Him like never before. Far too many of us avoid trouble at all costs. We spend our time and money on things to protect us from harm. There's nothing wrong with taking prudent measures to protect our families and ourselves, but Jesus calls us to "bring his kingdom to earth, as it is in heaven." That means we graciously share the gospel with unbelievers, we provide care for hurting people, give time and resources to help the needy, and fight against injustice in our communities and our nation. The compassion to care for others often can only be learned from our own experiences of finding God to be kind and near in times of suffering.

Risk is an essential ingredient in a life of extravagant devotion to God. Some of us are "adrenaline junkies" who love to live on the edge all the time. I'm not advocating that kind of lifestyle for most people, but all of us are called to get out of our comfort zones from time to time and do something great for God. Although no one can write a prescription for courageous faith that fits all of us, God will direct us to a hurting person or a desperate need at the right time. I've seen it again and again, and it's a glorious thing for the Spirit to lead us to step into someone's life to provide hope, truth, love, and resources at just the right moment.

> ## Sweet surrender means we love Jesus so much we truly want to obey Him.

When you become a Christian, you are adopted into God's family, but you are also enlisted in His army. Paul told Timothy to serve as a "good soldier" whose passion is to please his Commander. Being a soldier carries an inherent risk of danger and death. The crucial question always remains, "Is God worthy of my love and loyalty?" If the answer is "yes," He'll value your courage and availability, and He'll use you to do some amazing things in people's lives. You may prefer to stay safe in a cocoon of self-protection so as to avoid as many risks as possible, but you'll miss out on the *adventure* of the Christian life—and the spiritual muscle in your soul will slowly grow weak and flabby.

God's most courageous soldiers don't always look the way we picture warriors, yet as I've discovered, God sometimes uses those we consider weak to shame those who appear strong. So you can grasp what I'm talking about, I must share with you a story about one of the volunteers in God's army whose iron will to share the Gospel still inspires me every time I think about him.

> Scottie's mission trip was extravagant devotion in action.

Scottie is stricken with cerebral palsy. His contorted muscles allow such limited control and movement that he can only stagger precariously. To watch him walk is to fear that with every step, he'll topple to the ground. As a result, he spends most of his daily life confined to a wheelchair. The affliction inhibits his ability to communicate, rendering it nearly impossible to understand his slurred and fitful speech. Yet once when I called for participants in a short-term mission trip from our church to Ecuador, Scottie was among the first to volunteer. I wondered if he might have misunderstood what would be involved. The trip would entail an arduous journey into the backwoods of South America, the very region where famed missionary Jim Eliot had sacrificed his life to win indigenous tribes to Christ half a century ago.

"Scottie," I explained as gently as I could, "we'll be packing in on muddy trails. Your wheelchair just won't make it."

He looked me in the eye and said, "Pastor Bryan, my wheelchair may not make it, but *I will*."

Several members of my board cautioned me against allowing Scottie to make the trip. While I respected the wisdom of their counsel, I had seen the fire in Scottie's eye and could only say to my leadership team, "If you're convinced he shouldn't go, then you tell him. I won't."

No one told Scottie he couldn't go with us to Ecuador, and sure enough, his wheelchair gummed up on the first trail. But when we finally made it to our destination deep in the forest, the team from our church—and more importantly, the villagers for whom we were building a church—witnessed one of the most holy offerings to God we'd ever seen.

The most laborious and unforgiving task required for our construction work was the preparation of gravel for making concrete. We received it on site in piles of dirt from which the rocks had to be extracted for use, and every morning, Scottie would begin the workday by crawling spastically to the top of a mound. There he would lie in the rock and dirt using his better arm to separate one-by-one the stones so we could use them. For five days, ten hours a day, Scottie lay in 100-degree heat, hand-digging rocks out of dirt so God's people could have a church in the jungle. His bleeding fingers, knees, and elbows proclaimed a devotion to serving his Lord that captured the hearts of the South American tribes people—and our mission team—beyond anything else done or said that week.

The Old Testament offers a similarly moving example of God at work through human weakness. After the death of King Saul, his crippled son Mephibosheth is welcomed by David to live and dine with him in the palace. Although Mephibosheth couldn't walk, whenever he was seated at the king's table no one could tell he was crippled—being in the presence of the king made him as able as anyone else.

Scottie stands as a reminder of God's joy in using everyone committed to His purposes. Scottie's mission trip was extravagant devotion in action. His was *courageous faith*. As menial as his task was, my service seemed almost meaningless by comparison. I hold up his example to others and say, "Go, and do likewise."

Outrageous Generosity

In our consumer-driven society, advertisements make all sorts of promises, but the real message of every ad isn't that the product or service will give us a nice ride, help us lose weight, enable us to enjoy the latest software, or help us plan for retirement. The real promise is *ultimate fulfillment*: we simply can't be truly happy and content without buying the product!

If you think you're not affected by the pervasive messages of "more, bigger, and better," you need to reconsider. Professor Philip Kenneson has observed that it's easy for believers to think following Christ is simply one more consumer choice, to be valued or discarded as we desire. In his book, *Life on the Vine,* he writes:

> *Living in a culture like ours also encourages Christians to frame their understanding of faith primarily in terms of self-interest. (What's in it for me? . . .) Hence, many people are "converted" less out of their sense that they are estranged from God and other people and their desire to be reconciled, but more out of a sense that they're savvy consumers, knowing a good deal when they see one.*[23]

When we surrender our lives to Christ, one of the most important implications is that we are making a commitment to stop living according to the world's values. All around

---

23. Philip D. Kenneson, *Life on the Vine* (Downer's Grove, IL: Intervarsity Press, 1999), 47.

us, people strive to acquire more money, more stuff, more of "the good life," but a Christian's passion or consuming drive should be to use every available resource to honor Christ. That doesn't mean we sell everything we have, give it to the poor, and become hermits. Jesus asked only one person in Scripture to give away all that he had, and it was because that man valued his money too highly. For most of us, God primarily wants to change the decision-making grid in our minds.

> God wants to change the decision-making grid in our minds.

Many Christians secretly resent having to give any money at all to church or to any other charitable group. They operate with the attitude, "All this is mine, and, God, if I choose to give You any, You owe me!" A heart transformed by Jesus has the opposite perspective: "Lord, I'm all Yours, and everything I have is a gift from You. Do with it whatever You wish. Show me where You want me to invest Your money to expand Your kingdom."

One of the "trophies" in my office is a Mason jar containing $62.50. It represents to me an example of *outrageous generosity*. A nine-year-old boy in my congregation worried during the year I took no salary that my family might not survive, and he began praying every night that we would be all right. An artistic young man, he had been hand-drawing race cars on calendars and selling them for a dollar each. He intended to use the income from his calendar business to pay his own way to summer camp, but he began to sense God leading him otherwise. He had earned just over sixty dollars when he told his mother God wanted him to give his money to help me.

"God's going to take care of Pastor Bryan," his mother assured him, not wanting to see her son regret "losing" his hard-earned money.

But he persisted, and none of her arguments dissuaded him. Finally, a bit exasperated with his mother, he explained, "Mom, you've told me God speaks even to little kids, and He can use what I have to offer, no matter how young I might be. I believe He's telling me I'm one of the ways He wants to provide for Pastor and his family. This is one moment that, in my heart, I know what I'm supposed to do. Let me do this."

The next morning, he and his mom brought to my office at the church a mason jar containing $62.50. Outrageous generosity! Whether you're a nine-year-old boy or a ninety-year-old man, extravagant devotion includes acknowledging that everything you have is God's.

Each of us is simply a steward of the things with which God has entrusted us, and one day, we'll give an account of that stewardship. Whether it's trust, obedience, faith, or possessions, rightly devoted followers of Christ realize that anything we offer back to God is merely what He put into our hands to begin with.

Think Outside the Box

1. *What evidence do you have that your belief in Christ is not just "blind faith"?*
2. *Like the disciples in the boat with Jesus, have you ever experienced a time when you "should have known better" and trusted God more than you did?*
3. *I made the statement, "If you never sense Christ asking you to do something that makes you uncomfortable, it's questionable whether or not you're actually following Him." In light of this idea, to what degree are you following Jesus?*

4. *Have you ever balked at taking a particular step of faith because, as in the story of Naaman, it seemed too simple? Is there something facing you like that right now?*

5. *What are some ways you construct life so as to avoid the risk of failure? Who do you know that models courageous faith?*

6. *How did you feel as you read Scottie's story? Inspired? Sad? Ashamed? Encouraged? What made you feel that way?*

7. *How do you evaluate your Christian life in terms of self-interest?*

chapter 9

let it go!

We are forgetful people and need regular reminders to keep us on track. When Joshua led God's people across the Jordan River into the Promised Land, he ordered them to set up huge piles of rocks to commemorate the day. That way, for the rest of their lives they could reflect on a visual reminder of God's provision and leadership by which He took them into their new homeland.

God gives us many reminders of our need and His provision. At the Last Supper, Jesus told His disciples that the regular observance of this meal would retell of His sacrifice. "As often as you eat and drink it," He explained, "do this to remember Me."

I need to be drawn back again and again to the necessity of my own surrender to Christ. I must have a stake in the ground—something that reinforces my understanding of His grace and my ongoing commitment to complete trust, uncommon obedience, courageous faith, and outrageous generosity. Several years ago, I signed a ten-page contract with God. The first page says simply, "Yes, Lord." The other nine pages are blank. In normal business dealings, by contrast, all the specifications, responsibilities, and timelines are spelled out on multiple pages of a contract, and the parties to the agreement sign on the last page, perhaps with a notary's verification. We have attorneys draw up contracts on our behalf, and if someone else writes them, we have our lawyers scrutinize them to let us know what changes will be in our best interests. The clear point of the contract's structure is that the signers must understand all the details before they make a commitment.

Living a surrendered life to God every day, however, is different. It requires us to say "yes" to God with no qualifications or stipulations. The pages of my contract with Him are blank because He knows what needs to go there, and I submit to His sovereign will—no matter what. The contract is a solemn demonstration of my commitment to be His man, through good times and bad, in darkness and light, in life and in death. To be sure this obligation stays in front of me every day, I keep a plaque on my desk that says simply, "Yes, Lord."

> I keep a plaque on my desk that says simply, "Yes, Lord."

Are you willing to make this kind of contractual commitment to God?

Don't answer that question quickly or lightly. Pray, consider, and think about the benefits and sacrifices entailed in giving God a blanket "Yes!" for the rest of your life. This doesn't mean, of course, that you'll obey flawlessly all the time. We're fallible. Sometimes we'll fail and need God's forgiveness. But the contract is a bold statement of intent, a reminder that we've shifted the ownership of our lives to Someone who is far more competent than we will ever be. Are you in?

The old hymn below captures the essence of a "blank page" contract with God. If you're in, I suggest you use it as your prayer when you make your contract with the Lord. In my own journey of surrender, these words have become the anthem of my heart:

" 'Tis so sweet to trust in Jesus,

102

Just to take Him at His Word;
Just to rest upon His promise,
And to know, "Thus saith the Lord!"

Refrain:
Jesus, Jesus, how I trust Him!
How I've proved Him o'er and o'er;
Jesus, Jesus, precious Jesus!
Oh, for grace to trust Him more!

I'm so glad I learned to trust Thee,
Precious Jesus, Savior, Friend;
And I know that Thou art with me,
Wilt be with me to the end."[24]

Housing Allowance

Sometimes contracts need to be renewed. As I said, we tend to be forgetful people. And much to my chagrin, I discovered that "we" even includes me. You'd think after giving up my salary for a year at God's request and starving myself in search of His direction, I'd have realized the cost of truly surrendering to His will. You'd also think I'd never forget His faithfulness in responding to my devotion. But think again, because God had to repeat the lesson for me.

A few years after my no-salary period, God led me to a church on the north side of Dallas. Situated in a nice suburb, the church had a rich mission heritage, a wonderful reputation, and plenty of well-to-do, white-collar people. Once in Texas, I reflected on my struggles at the Pine Bluff church and concluded that the call to this more comfortable ministry was God's way of rewarding me for my radical obedience and sacrifice. It made perfect sense. Now God could trust me completely to keep Him first in my life. He'd

---

24. Louisa M. R. Stead, " 'Tis So Sweet to Trust in Jesus," 1882.

provided wonderfully in my new situation so I wouldn't have to worry or be challenged about finances here.

I was wrong. And the seeds for my new level of spiritual exercise were planted even before I left Arkansas.

The move from Pine Bluff wasn't without drama. Because we had lived without a salary for a year, Haley and I were renting a mobile home. One of the resulting adventures happened after Haley had traveled with me to speak in Denver at a denominational convention of 20,000 preachers and other church leaders. While we were gone, an animal crawled between the floor and the sub-floor of our mobile home and died. Our revulsion at the stench was surpassed only by the horror of having several million blowflies in our home. As soon as we opened the door, Haley and I looked at each other and cried. Then we laughed. Sometimes, that's all you can do when life gets so absurd. The divine irony is that only 24 hours earlier, I had been speaking to thousands at the Pepsi Center in Denver. Now I was dodging flies and trying not to gag on the smell that greeted our arrival home.

An advantage to our down-sized, mobile home living, however, became apparent when the moving company arrived to pick up our things for the move to Dallas. The movers were shocked to see that we had almost nothing of value. Our home looked like it had been furnished with stuff Goodwill didn't even want. The workers withheld comment on the smell that still lingered in our house, but they did seem to work especially quickly that day. It got our move off to an efficient start.

Although we had sold everything of value in our house, Haley and I managed to hang onto a few real estate investments. We liquidated these properties and bought what to us at the time was our dream home in Texas. The same moving crew that pulled away from a mobile home in Pine Bluff drove up to the front door of a handsome, new

5,000-square-foot house in Dallas. They must have been impressed with the upgrade in our circumstances because I overheard one of them say to another, "Dude, we're in the wrong business."

The change in living standard wasn't lost on our children, either. Six-year-old son Gavyn walked into the foyer of the house and eyed the 20-foot ceiling. His voice echoed in the open space as he turned to me and asked, "Dad, is this a hotel? Are we on vacation, or do we really get to live here?"

The Spirit continued, "Bryan, it's not a season. It's a lifestyle."

"No, son, we're not just visiting," I assured him. "God has given us this place to live."

I loved seeing the look of joy and relief on Haley's face as we walked around the house that day. I was thrilled to give her the home she deserved, and we thanked God for providing so well for us. Settling into the new place delighted our trailer-weary hearts.

A few weeks after arriving in Texas, I flew to Nebraska to speak at the church of a dear friend, and during the trip, I read a book about sacrifice and obedience this friend had given me. In a moment of reflection on the flight home, God whispered to me, "I want you to give me the most valuable possession you have."

"Lord, let's hit rewind here!" I snapped back at Him in my heart. "I haven't been getting paychecks consistently for very long, thanks to what I've done for You. In Pine Bluff, I did exactly what You asked me to do. I came through that season. I've already passed that test!"

Undeterred, the Spirit continued, "Bryan, it's not a season. It's a lifestyle."

I thought for a few seconds—all the time it took for me to realize that the most valuable thing (the *only* valuable thing) we owned was our new house. Since we had invested every dime we could get our hands on to buy it, I slammed the door shut on my conversation with the Lord.

"I'm not even going to tell Haley about this conversation," I chided Him. "She's been through enough."

For several months, I kept this message from God secluded in my heart and out of my consciousness. Then, at a missions conference, God reminded me of His clear leading on the plane home from Nebraska. The central message at one of the sessions was *surrender*. Pastors streamed to the front of the auditorium to weep and pray. At last, I realized my time had come—again.

> With tears streaming down her face, she told me, "Bryan, God wants our house."

I fell on my face in the aisle and laid out my worries, "Lord, I'm going to need several confirmations from you about this decision. We've only lived in the house for a few months!"

When the conference was over, everyone left the building, but I just sat there weeping. I worried about the pain I would put Haley and the kids through again if I acted on what I knew God wanted me to do. Our boys had just started adjusting to a new public school in the community, and if we had to move, they might be ripped out of their schools to attend one somewhere else. And Haley . . . I hated to think about the anguish losing her dream home would cause.

John Cruz, our church's executive pastor who was also attending the conference, saw me and walked over to my seat. His prophetic gifts were in gear that night as he said quietly, "Pastor, for two weeks, the Lord has given me a message for you, but it didn't seem to make sense. My wife and I saw you struggling in the service tonight, and she asked if I'd given you the word God told me to give you. 'You have to tell him,' she said. So Pastor, I don't know what's bothering you, but the Holy Spirit has been telling me for two weeks: Whatever He has told you to do, do it."

All I could do was nod my head.

I hadn't ever told Haley about the Spirit's instructions on my Nebraska trip or my nagging struggle with obedience—and I didn't tell her about John's word from the Lord. If she was going to get the message, I decided, it had to come straight from God.

After John relayed God's message to me that night, Haley and I joined several other pastors and their wives for dinner. We got back to the hotel late, and as we stood in the bathroom brushing our teeth, she turned to me and asked, "What are you thinking? You've got a strange look in your eye. Is God telling you something?"

I replied, "I don't think so. I hope not." I paused a few seconds, then blurted, "But if He is, He's going to tell you, too. If He doesn't say anything to you, we're okay."

We went to bed, and after a little while, Haley got up. "Honey, where are you going?" I wondered.

She looked at me thoughtfully before answering. "I'm going to pray. I can't stand the thought that our entire future hinges on whether or not I'm listening to God."

An hour and a half later, she came out of the bathroom and woke me up. With tears streaming down her face, she told me, "Bryan, God wants our house."

The rest of the night, we talked about how we'd give our house away. We knew people would ask why in the world we would do such a thing, and we wanted to give them a good answer.

Several months later, we were ready and knew exactly how to communicate what we were up to. We rented the 10,000-seat Garland Events Center where we designated 3,000 seats for the people we expected from our congregation and taped the names of 7,000 family members, friends, and co-workers on the other seats. During the service, congregation members began to read the names, and I explained that someday those seats wouldn't be empty. They would be filled with men and women, boys and girls who had come to Christ through the ministry of the people in our church. But, I went on, to have this kind of impact, we need to demonstrate complete trust, uncommon obedience, courageous faith, and outrageous generosity.

As a first-fruit offering to that end, Haley and I asked representatives of a title company to come forward, and there in front of everyone, we deeded our house to the church. I explained that the corporate dream to reach the people we love for Christ is much bigger than the personal dream for Haley and me to have a comfortable home. We were committed to live for the bigger dream—and so was our entire family.

Let the Little Children Come—and Give

If you're a parent, you have a special opportunity to influence a few, hand-picked others for Christ. The measure of devotion you model for your children will position them for a lifetime of faithfulness. Your outrageous generosity and courageous, uncommon obedience will shape the faith of your children. A week before the service at which we deeded our house to the church, Haley gave me an assignment: tell the boys we're giving away our house.

As if to make the task almost simple, Cadyn came into my room one night while I was studying for a message. He announced, "Daddy, I found ten dollars in my backpack I didn't know I had. I believe Jesus put it there."

"Why do you think that, son?" I asked.

"Because the other day, I gave five dollars to a missionary, and I think Jesus put the ten dollars back in there to multiply my gift."

His smile, though, quickly changed to a look of confusion. "But, Dad," he went on, "I have a problem. I think Jesus wants me to give this ten dollars, too." He paused, then looked me in the eye. "Dad, I'm only eight years old. How am I supposed to know what to do when Jesus asks for everything?"

Talk about a teachable moment! I pulled him up to sit on the bed with me and explained that in a week, his mom and I were going to give our house to the church.

> Your courageous, uncommon obedience will shape the faith of your children.

He stared thoughtfully at me and asked, "Does that include my bedroom, too?"

"Yes, son," I told him. "Your bedroom, too."

As the idea registered with him, tears began to run down his face. He thought hard for a minute, and then, unshaken, he looked at me. "Daddy, I don't know where we're going to live, but I know this: Jesus is going to take care of our family. Would you mind if I give my ten dollars when you and Mom give the house?"

My heart nearly exploded. "Yes, son. That would be fine. Jesus will be thrilled with your gift."

A few days later on the Saturday night before the momentous Sunday service, the Lord showed me that my son had more faith than I did. The Spirit whispered, "Bryan, I want you to give me everything. Hold nothing back."

As had become my custom, I instantly retaliated, "Lord, I'm about to give you everything! What more could you want?"

Suddenly, I realized my son truly was going to give all that was his. As monumental as the house giveaway seemed to Haley and me, we still had the money in our checking and savings accounts, but now I sensed God moving me to give that, too.

"So that's it!" I told God. "You want every cent. You want us to start our financial life over tomorrow morning."

I didn't even want to look at Haley. How could I tell her we were going to become both homeless *and* penniless in the same day? While she was reading her Bible in the bedroom that night, I avoided eye contact, but I asked, "God didn't say anything to you lately, did He?"

Without looking at me, she said emphatically, "Yes, Bryan. You can give it all."

We got up and went to the computer to check our bank accounts. The next morning, we gave our house, every dime we had in the world, and our son's ten dollars. I walked out of the Garland Event Center a penniless pauper, but I expected God to bless our family in incredible ways. You probably won't be surprised at this point to have me say that I wasn't disappointed. God provided a new place to live, and we never missed a meal. Besides the family blessings we experienced during the following six months, our church paid off all of its debt. We were in the sweet spot between the trapezes again—and loving it.

Think Outside the Box

1. *Do you need to draw up or renew a contract with God?*
2. *Is God asking you to do something right now to which you simply need to say, "Yes, Lord"?*

3. *Does the story about giving away the house near Dallas inspire you? Scare you? Repulse you?*

4. *What are you involved in—preferably in your local church—that represents a bigger dream than your own self-interest? If there's nothing, you probably need to be on the lookout for something more God wants of you.*

5. *Are you holding out on God, not wanting to give Him everything in some area of your life? If so, what is keeping you from letting go?*

chapter 10

security check

I once shared the concepts of this book in a special presentation to seminarians. In response, Harold, a student from Guatemala, commented to the group:

> *The difference between believers in my country and the ones in America is that we have different funnels. Americans preach about the greatness of God in church and at conferences—that's the wide part at the top of your funnel. But at the bottom, where people live, you don't trust Him to do much at all. At the bottom, your funnel is very narrow. In Guatemala, our God is as big at the bottom of our funnel as He is at the top. We trust Him to do great things every day. Americans value security over spiritual vitality, and it causes your faith to be anemic and weak. If you want to see God do great things, you have to enlarge the bottom of your funnel to let His Spirit flow. You have to increase your capacity for God.*

Harold's insight launched me into serious reflection about the cult of security to which all too many believers in our country belong. It's a cult(ure) that finds its sense of well-being in things like earning as large and consistent a salary as possible and living in a lovely home of our own. I've come to the conclusion—the sad and painful conclusion—

that Harold is exactly right. We American Christians talk big, but we live little. We're afraid to take any risk to trust God that might result in failure or loss. Although few of us recognize our plight, we desperately need to increase the capacity for God in our lives. To do that, though, we need to be ruthlessly honest about our misplaced priority on safety over cultivating a genuine thirst for God.

The Whole Pie

One of the main reasons for spiritual weakness in our country is that we've compartmentalized our faith. For many of us, spiritual life exists only for an hour on Sunday morning and perhaps a few minutes each morning before we run out the door to engage "the real world." We've developed a sacred-secular dichotomy, with disastrous results. Our "relationship with God" becomes a filling station where we go once in a while to top off our spiritual tanks. Then we run along on our own without a thought about God until the next time we need a refill.

A number of solid Christian thinkers recognize the danger of compartmentalization in our lives. They share a common observation that we seem to have three linear priorities: God, family, and work. We treat these as separate items on life's menu of priorities. After we've worshipped on Sunday morning, had a daily devotional, or attended a small group, we "close the book" and move on to the next thing, either family or work. But we don't take God with us to those other compartments. Each slice of life has little to do with the others, and in fact, we do our best to be sure they are separate and "balanced." This way, we can enthusiastically raise our hands in worship on Sunday morning, then rip someone off in a business deal the next day without a twinge of guilt. We can feel close to God in our devotions but get up and swear at the kids a few minutes later.

Living like this doesn't mesh with God's extravagance. Instead of seeing our relationship with the Master as just one piece of life's pie, we need to see Him as the crust that holds it all together. It's not even good enough to regard God as the biggest piece of the pie. If we see Him that way, we'll still leave Him out of the rest of our lives. The "pie crust" of God's love, power, and truth is the foundation for everything we do. To be fully devoted to Him, we have to trust Him to guide us as we work, while driving the car, in managing our children, in every personal relationship, as we handle our money, when we face temptation to gossip about a friend, and everything else we do each day.

We never stop belonging to the One Who created and redeemed us.

If we see Jesus as one piece of our lives, we only let Him speak to us about worship in isolated "spiritual" times. We won't listen for Him to inspire or challenge us to be His man or His woman the rest of the week. When He's just a piece of the pie, we feel safe from any serious demands He might make on us. Compartmentalizing allows us to protect the rest of our lives from God instead of offering it all to Him. We need to realize we never stop belonging to the One who created and redeemed us. We eat, sleep, work, and play with our Father who loves us, directs us, and gives us responsibilities to fulfill. Worship is a heart devoted to God all day, every day. It's not church—it's life!

As a pastor, I believe I'm the coach, and people in our church the players. Our game doesn't just happen on Sunday morning. It starts there and runs through the rest of the week. When we gather on Sunday, it's a praise rally and strategy session. Consider how ridiculous it would be if a coach fired up his team before the Super Bowl, only to have them file out of the locker room, stroll to their cars, and drive home instead of charging onto the field to play the big game. But that's what happens to most people after church—they miss the chance to be champions for Christ throughout the week.

Security as a Prison

When I read through the Bible, it's obvious that the people God applauded are those who found the courage to take bold risks for Him. They didn't play it safe. In the face of old age and impending impotence, Abraham and Sarah trusted God to provide a son. Joseph endured until he attained a position in which God used him to rescue his family from starvation. Hebrews 11 is a catalog of such men and women who faced daunting obstacles but trusted God to do the miraculous. In many cases, God worked in ways that were almost unbelievable, but even when He didn't, the epitaph of the ones who died is that "the world was not worthy of them." A spiritual jailbreak changes our values and relationships; it gives us a new perspective on our money and our time, and gives God the opportunity to honor the act extravagantly. I've seen people break out of this prison in remarkable ways.

116

Lisel listened with ears and heart the Sunday morning I announced that Haley and I would give our house and all our money to the church for God's Kingdom purposes. A high school senior, this young woman had already established a lifestyle of following Christ faithfully. She was also an athlete whose greatest personal dream at the time was to play soccer for Texas A & M University. Although of ordinary means, Lisel's parents hoped to help her achieve that dream and had spent years saving money little by little to pay for their daughter's college education. But that Sunday morning, God spoke to Lisel, and she whispered to her parents, "I really believe God wants me to give my future away and trust Him. My college. I want to give away what you've saved for my college."

Lisel believed the Lord was calling her to give up her college fund of nearly $20,000. Afraid that such a move would devastate their daughter's long-term prospects by depriving her of a college education, to say nothing of the chance to play soccer at Texas A & M or any other school, her parents convinced her to talk it over and pray with them about her leading during the coming week. There might be the potential she could receive scholarship support, but to

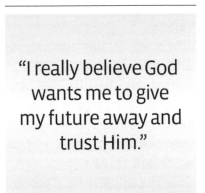

"I really believe God wants me to give my future away and trust Him."

that point, only a few small schools had even bothered to respond to their inquiries.

During the family's week of prayer about Lisel's leading, all three of them became convinced that they should take the step of obedience and give the college fund to church. So on Sunday morning, July 16th, Lisel and her parents walked to the front of the church, sobbing in joy and relief that they had heard clearly from God. Carrying with them a check donating 100 percent of the college fund, they held nothing back, trusting only that this was the offering God asked of them. It was a gut-wrenching break from the prison of security, surpassed only by what God offered in response.

On Monday morning, July 17th, Lisel's high school soccer coach received a phone call from the coach at Texas A & M, offering Lisel a scholarship to play soccer at the school of her dreams. Up to that point, there had been no communication whatsoever from the school, yet here, within

24 hours of Lisel's faithful sacrifice, was God's extravagant response. Although it wasn't a "full ride," it opened the door wide enough for Lisel to start school. It also gave God a chance to continue showing Himself faithful. Lisel's parents have since shared numerous stories of how the Lord has provided for Lisel's every need while in school.

Values

When we value security over extravagant devotion, we refuse to take risks. We only do those things that offer guaranteed results—or maybe ones where failure can be pinned on someone else. Our highest goal is to keep from looking foolish. We engage in image management, making sure people think well of us, and we seldom even consider what God thinks of us.

118

The apostle Paul models what it looks like to put God's opinion before that of other men. In a theological and cultural conflict over the nature of the gospel, the apostle stood strong against his opposition. He pointed out to the Galatians the way to think: "Am I now trying to win the approval of men, or of God? Or am I trying to please men? If I were still trying to please men, I would not be a servant of Christ" (Galatians 1:10). Paul was committed to Jesus and His truth, no matter what anyone thought of him. He was willing to take great risks for God.

God wants us to believe Him for things that are so large, so audacious, that if He doesn't show up we'll fall flat on our faces. This isn't a guarantee that everything will always work out perfectly, and it doesn't mean we can take foolish risks and expect God's blessing. It does mean, though, that we need to look in the Bible to see what God truly values and the kind of people He applauds, and we need to pray with an open heart, "Lord, I'm Yours, and I want what You want. Show me what You want me to do. Challenge me; use me. Like Caleb, I'm telling You, Lord, 'Give me that mountain!'"

I believe God is looking for people who will step out of their comfort zones and make plans so big and pray so specifically that they will look foolish if God doesn't show up. Dwight L. Moody, one of the great pastors in the history of Chicago and our country, was a man gripped with God's calling on his life. He often told people, "It remains to be seen what God will do with a man who gives himself up wholly to him."[25] He always quickly completed the thought by saying, "Well, I will be that man."

In a private conversation with the noted pastor and theologian, R. A. Torrey, Moody remarked, "Torrey, if I believed that God wanted me to jump out of that window, I would jump."

Torrey later reflected, "I believe he would. If he thought God wanted him to do anything, he would do it. He belonged wholly, unreservedly, unqualifiedly, entirely, to God."[26]

Being that kind of person is worth the risk.

Think Outside the Box

1. *How does compartmentalizing faith into "one piece of life's pie" erode spiritual vitality? How can you tell if a person has that perspective about life? Are there things you compartmentalize?*
2. *Do you really believe you are God's partner in the great enterprise of building and establishing His Kingdom on earth? Why or why not?*
3. *To what degree is security a prison for you?*
4. *What did you think of Lisel's story? Foolish? Unrealistic? Exciting? Inspiring?*

---

25. Cited by Shelton L. Smith in *Great Preaching on Christ* (Sword of the Lord Publishers, 1ST edition, 2002), 126.
26. R. A. Torrey, "Why God Used D. L. Moody," cited at www.wholesomewords.org/biography/biomoody6.html.

5. *I noted in this chapter that "God wants us to believe Him for things that are so large, so audacious, that if He doesn't show up we'll fall flat on our faces." Is there anything gigantic you are—or should be—believing God for right now?*

6. *Think about D. L. Moody's statement, "It remains to be seen what God will do with a man who gives himself up wholly to Him." He wanted to be that person. Do you? If not, what stands in your way?*

chapter 11

security clearance

When security is our highest value, the circle of our lives is reduced to a dot. We constantly worry about what others think about us, and we wear masks to be sure we manage our public image. Soon, we don't even know who we are anymore because we've been projecting someone we're not for so long. Because we hide behind our masks and aren't honest with each other, our relationships are shallow. As consumers, we come to church to get what we want, but we aren't willing to invest in each other.

The early church would be aghast at this development. First-century Christians understood what it meant to be "the Body of Christ," interdependent on one another and thriving in community. There was friction, of course. That always happens when fallen people try to love one another, but the believers were known throughout the Roman world as people willing to sacrifice for each other. During two times of plague in the first centuries after Christ, about one-fourth of the empire became deathly ill. Pagans fled for their lives, even abandoning their own family members. Christians, however, had compassion for their family and friends as well as the sick pagans. They cared for them, in spite of the risk to themselves. As a result, countless people came to Christ because believers risked their own health to reach out and care for others in a time of need.[27]

---

27. Described by Rodney Stark in *The Rise of Christianity* (HarperOne, 1997).

In our culture, most of us live in suburbia where we can avoid needy people in the cities. We build tall privacy fences—literally and figuratively—to protect us from the outside world. We enter and leave our homes from the seclusion of our garages, using automatic door openers so no interaction with our neighbors is necessary. We ride to work alone in our cars next to thousands of others who are alone in their cars. At work, we sit in isolated cubicles, working on our own projects. Air conditioning that we think of as a necessity keeps us inside so we no longer sit on porches with neighbors to talk about life. Yet we compare our lives to everyone around us. If we're winning the comparison game, we feel superior. If we're losing, shame grips us. We are lonely, broken, and hurting, but we don't want anybody to know about our pain. We don't want to take the risk of being honest because the chance of being hurt again is too great. Biblical community is messy, but when we show the love of Jesus to others, it's a beautiful and powerful thing, and, unlike masks, it transforms lives.

> "We're going to live better on a blessed 90 percent than a selfish 100."

The masks that we wear often have their source in some surprising "values" we hold too dear, and they interfere with our ability to finally clear the security trap. Two particular barriers make it difficult for many Americans to open up to others.

(1) The Money Barrier
Many of us are afraid to tithe because we're terrified we won't have enough money to buy the things that keep us comfortable. We miss the point that God isn't asking for a

tithe because He needs our money. He owns "the cattle on a thousand hills." He's the Lord over all creation. Scripture explains over and over that giving tests the condition of our hearts. Jesus said, "Where your treasure is, there will your heart be also" (Matthew 6:21). God wants to pour out His blessings on us, but first, He tests us to see if our hearts belong to Him. When we cling to our money instead of offering it gladly and generously to Him, we turn off the valve of His blessing. Our preference for financial security actually results in monetary and spiritual poverty.

Some people have heard me talk about the tithe, and they say, "Isn't the tithe an Old Testament principle? Since we're no longer under the law but under grace, it doesn't apply anymore."

When I hear that, more often than not I suspect people are looking for a way out of giving what they know they should. While it's true we live under grace, the tithe is the beginning point of giving, a benchmark of the minimum given by someone who is thrilled with the grace of God. In fact, in the New Testament, our response shouldn't be, "God, I'm giving you 10 percent," but "God, everything I have is yours, and I'm thrilled for you to use it in any way you want."

My mother taught me all I needed to know about God blessing our tithe. When I was a rebellious teen and she was a single mom, she always wrote the first check after payday to the church. Sometimes as I watched her, I asked in a tone of exasperation, "Mom, we don't even know if we can pay our bills. Why are you giving your hard-earned money to the church?"

She always smiled and told me, "Son, we're going to live better on a blessed 90 percent than a selfish 100."

(2) The Time Barrier

We also guard our time. According to sociologists, as recently as a few years ago, the average person had ten hours of discretionary time each week, but today, in a world brimming with "time-saving devices," we have less than two.[28] We commute longer to work, and kids participate in so many after-school activities that parents spend much of their time behind the wheel of their cars. Dinner is a quick drive-thru before the next practice or game. In the little time we have left, we resent demands anyone would put on us—especially God. After all, we're giving all we've got all week. How could He want more?

> God longs to give us more freedom, joy, and purpose than we ever imagined.

Like the proverbial frog in a kettle, the heat of expectations of "the good life" keeps getting higher, but we don't notice that we're being boiled. We look around at all the people pursuing the American Dream, and we conclude that we have to keep up. We drive two (nice) cars, buy a bigger house than we can afford, put vacations on credit, rush from event to event, and wonder why we don't have much passion for God. When we pray, we ask God to help us fulfill our self-focused goals of success, pleasure, and approval, but God doesn't seem to be answering like we hoped.

We can't live an extravagant life of devotion if God is just an add-on to the American Dream, or worse, if we see Him as a tool to help us attain it. At the beginning of his book, *The Purpose Driven Life*, Pastor Rick Warren throws

---

28. From a presentation by Mel Ming, founder of Leadership Development Resources, "Congregational Realities," November 2003.

down the gauntlet: "It's not about you. It's about him."[29] We tend to get that reversed, but as long as we insist on using God instead of loving and obeying Him, we'll stay locked in the prison of misplaced expectations. We'll value safety and security over radical devotion to Him. In *The Divine Conspiracy,* author and professor Dallas Willard observes:

> *No one need worry about our getting the best of God in some bargain with Him, or that we might somehow succeed in using Him for our purposes. Anyone who thinks this is a problem has seriously underestimated the intelligence and agility of our Father in the heavens. He will not be tricked or cheated.*[30]

God longs to give us more freedom, joy, and purpose than we ever imagined, but if we insist on playing it safe, we'll stay stuck in the prison of lowered hopes and little passion. It may sound strange, but a prison is actually a pretty safe place to be. The people there don't have to worry about the ups and downs of the stock market. They're not concerned about the weather or whether they'll be fed that day. Healthcare is provided, and they get free haircuts. A lot of the risks of life are gone, but so are the joys, thrills, and freedom to be who God has made you to be.

Getting Through Security

We've addressed four different areas of tasting and testing in these chapters on security: how we handle our values, our relationships, our money, and our time. It's all great in theory but doesn't get us anywhere until we put into action what we know. The psalmist invites people to "taste and

---

29. Rick Warren, *The Purpose Driven Life* (Grand Rapids: Zondervan, 2002), 17.
30. Dallas Willard, *The Divine Conspiracy* (HarperOne, 1998), 38.

see that the Lord is good" (Psalm 34:8). Every time we put a bite of a new food in our mouths, it's a test—of the cook's skill, of the quality of the ingredients, and of our palates. God wants us to take steps of faith, to taste His goodness— and test ourselves to see if we're really sold out to Him.

Complete trust in God is displayed through tangible acts of faith. The Bible provides numerous stories of coura- geous faith that sets miracles in motion. At a pivotal point in the nation of Israel, for example, God's people were in big trouble. The Philistines had been attacking, and King Saul hadn't been able to fend them off. To make matters worse, his "army" was only a ragtag bunch of men armed with farm tools. The enemy had imposed its will on God's people and set the Israelites up for failure. The Philistines had made it impossible for Saul's men to prepare for war: "Not a blacksmith could be found in the whole land of Israel, because the Philistines had said, 'Otherwise the Hebrews will make swords or spears!'...So on the day of the battle not a soldier with Saul and Jonathan had a sword or spear in his hand; only Saul and his son Jonathan had them" (1 Samuel 13:19, 22). The military and political situation was desperate.

As Saul's youthful son, Jonathan, looked at the situa- tion, he must have had conflicting emotions. He was well aware that he and his father's men were undermanned and pitifully armed, but he refused to give up. Through a bold, secret plan, he invited his armor-bearer to join him in a two-man assault on an impregnable position surrounded by cliffs! In a display of incomparable faith and cour- age, Jonathan encouraged him, "Come, let's go over to the outpost of those uncircumcised fellows. Perhaps the Lord will act in our behalf. Nothing can hinder the Lord from saving, whether by many or by few". The armor-bearer was inspired by Jonathan's courage and replied, "Do all that you have in mind. Go ahead; I am with you heart and soul" (1 Samuel 14:6-7).

The two men scaled a cliff and attacked the Philistine garrison, killing about 20 men. God, in turn, honored their audacious faith: "Then panic struck the whole {Philistine} army—those in the camp and field, and those in the out-posts and raiding parties—and the ground shook. It was a panic sent by God" (1 Samuel 14:15).

Saul's lookouts saw the enemy melt away from their fortress, so he ordered an attack by his few troops. By the time they arrived on the battlefield, the confused Philistines were attacking

> Complete trust in God is displayed through tangible acts of faith.

each other. Soon, more Israelite men joined the fight, and the rout was on. All day, Saul's tiny army chased and killed the mighty Philistines. How did it happen? Because one man looked beyond the despair of the situation and saw a trapeze bar of faith that could change history. He let go of his personal security to grasp God's way of delivering the enemy. And let's not forget the armor-bearer who showed at least as much courage as Jonathan. In fact, he may have demonstrated even greater courage because he was will-ing to follow Jonathan into what appeared to be a hopeless and deadly fight—and he didn't even have a sword of his own! Both men knew there were no guarantees, only belief that God would prevail through them. Jonathan had been completely honest when he said, "*Perhaps* the Lord will act in our behalf."

When situations are impossible, the setting is right for a miracle. If we orchestrate our lives to avoid risk, we prevent the very condition that's essential for a miracle—

abject, stark, unavoidable need. God has to take us to the end of our resources before we'll trust Him to deliver us to our destiny—with no Plan B and no other alternatives.

Too often, we begin our analysis of a situation by focusing on our fears, so we are paralyzed from the outset. Instead, we should model ourselves after Jonathan and rivet our hearts on God's character and the possibility that He just might work a miracle for us. With him, we say, "Perhaps God will act." In every bold act of faith I've ever made, I had to look beyond the doubts, excuses, and external criticisms—beyond what was secure to my eyes—and consider what God might do if my faith set Him free to be Himself. Often, I heard murmurs from people who wondered, "What if it's not from God?" But each time, I replied, "But what if it *is*?" I'd rather be bold to taste God's goodness and greatness, and see what happens, than to live in fearful mediocrity all my life. At those crucial moments in my life, I've had to think through the consequences of the risk, but also the consequences of not taking the risk. At the end of my life, I don't want to look back and lament that I "missed the moment." Even if I trust God but fall flat on my face, I want to be able to say, "I gave God all I've got." I want to be a Jonathan.

128

Think Outside the Box

1. *Where does your security lie?*
2. *Do you believe you can live better on a blessed 90 percent than on a tightly held 100 percent?*
3. *Does your time seem to evaporate before everything's done? Keep a time log for a week and see if the priorities of what you do with your life need to change.*
4. *Which of the barriers to clearing the need for security out of your life is the most challenging for you?*

5. *Like Jonathan and his armor-bearer, is there a tangible act of faith you need to make in order to unleash God's work in your life?*
6. *Do you make your decisions based on faith or on your fears?*

faith on the line

I love stories of war heroes and people who exhibit courage in the face of danger, perhaps because most of us don't ever experience situations like these. Our task for God, though, requires its own measure of bravery. For you, the trapeze bar of risk and hope may be to find the courage to open your mouth and tell a friend about Jesus. Or it may require you to listen to someone who truly annoys you, to care for someone who can give nothing in return, or to forgive someone who has deeply wounded you. God may lead someone to leave a secure career and start a business, plant a church, or become a missionary. We seldom read about such acts in history books, but they are the stuff of an extravagant spiritual life—and they bring joy to God's heart.

Substitutes for God

Our misplaced longing for security keeps us from putting our faith on the line and acting with the courage that elicits God's extravagance. The human heart often chooses the wrong objects of affection. We focus our hopes on things that were never meant to fill our hearts and satisfy our deepest desires.

Centuries ago, Augustine addressed the problem of "disordered loves." He noted that it's not wrong to love beauty, pleasure, people, and success, but it's tragically wrong if we love them more than we love God. He famously said, "You have made us for yourself, O Lord, and our hearts are restless until they rest in you."[31] We spend enormous amounts of time and money pursuing peripheral things instead of the primary thing, and the consequences of our misguided adventures are devastating.

Some of our pursuits are blatantly sinful. We lie, steal, cheat, and gossip to get what we want. We use substances and behaviors to numb the pain of abuse or nagging emptiness, and we engage in behaviors that promise momentary pleasure and relief. Not all of us are alcoholics or drug addicts. Far more of us have allowed our hearts to get preoccupied with the thrill of gambling, the quest of shopping, the comfort of food, the drive to get ahead in our careers, or the compulsion to build our retirement accounts. Many of us whose families are out of control think others in the family are the problem, so we set about trying to control their behavior, and all the while the main trouble is in our own hearts.

> No matter what we substitute for God, the result is the same: a life that is no life at all.

Using substances and unhealthy patterns to relieve pain and fill the emptiness of the heart isn't just a theory to me. As I explained in the testimony about my teenage years, life revolved around getting and using alcohol to numb the pain of a dysfunctional childhood. I didn't just dabble in addiction and the full corollary of lies and manipulation it brings. I was up to my eyeballs in it, and it threatened to destroy my life. No matter what we substitute for God, though, the result is the same: a life that is no life at all.

132

---

31. Augustine, *Confessions* I, 1.

Through the prophet Jeremiah, God shares what He thinks about our pursuit of sinful things instead of Him. When the people of God worshipped other gods (and that's what it means when we put substances, behaviors, or things where only God should be in our lives), He lamented:

> *My people have committed two sins:*
> *They have forsaken me,*
> *the spring of living water,*
> *and have dug their own cisterns,*
> *broken cisterns that cannot hold water.*
> *(Jeremiah 2:13)*

A cistern (for those of you who grew up in the city) collects rainwater for future use. The inert vessel has no natural flow, so it cannot replenish itself. God's complaint about His people was that they turned their backs on Him, the source of continuous, pure, refreshing, living water, and they foolishly worked hard to dig holes that hold only stagnant water. And even these cisterns were cracked and leaky. No wonder pursuing satisfaction any way other than God can't satisfy the longings of our hearts! The things we pour into our souls not only stagnate but leak out. We have to keep adding putrid water if we're to stay filled with anything at all.

God's complaint wasn't the final story for His people. Through the rest of Jeremiah's warning, the Lord explains that putting anything other than Him in the center of their hearts is idolatry—no laughing matter. Although the people protested God's harsh assessment, He used another metaphor to drive His point home:

> *How can you say, "I am not defiled;*
> *I have not run after the Baals?"*
> *See how you behaved in the valley;*

consider what you have done.
You are a swift she-camel
running here and there,
a wild donkey accustomed to the desert,
sniffing the wind in her craving—
in her heat who can restrain her?   Any males
that pursue her need not tire
themselves; at mating time they will find
her. (Jeremiah 2:23-24)

In our headlong demand for security and significance apart from God, we're like a she-camel or a female donkey in heat, looking for someone to satisfy us!

Is this too harsh? Is He really talking about the people of God? The human heart is desperately wicked, and until we go to be with the Lord, we'll be tempted to put lesser things—even blatantly sinful quests—in the center of our hearts.

When Good Things Get in the Way

As bad as blatant sin is, most of us face a more insidious problem in our relationship with God. Our disordered love isn't for sinful behaviors, but we've made good things, the gifts of God, into *essential* things. As Paul described in his letter to the Romans, we worship created things instead of the Creator (1:18-25). In our affluent culture (including even those of us with modest means who enjoy a level of comfort and technological sophistication that would have astounded a wealthy person a century ago), we don't see the normal conveniences of life as gifts from God. We are convinced it's our right to have them, and we're quite upset when we have to endure even the slightest hitch in our comforts. We acquire more and more things and increase our status and wealth. Everything, we secretly assume, is meant to get better and better for us—especially for the people of God. We live with an unexamined sense that we are entitled to "have it good."

Sooner or later, though, God puts His finger on even the "good" things that have taken His rightful place in our hearts. He may use a feather, or He may use a sledgehammer, but He makes sure to get our attention. If we're wise, we pay attention to the drift of our hearts and make whatever mid-course corrections are needed.

The wife of a friend of mine loves beautiful things and has decorated her home exquisitely. She realizes, however, that she has a tendency to get too wrapped up in beauty, so from time to time, she tests herself by attacking her temptation. She gives away paintings, vases, prized pieces of furniture, and other cherished possessions whenever they seem to be taking too strong a hold on her heart. My friend is sometimes shocked by his wife's choices. "They seem," he once told me, "a little too valuable to just give away."

> "It has to be something I love before giving it away can be a statement of devotion to God."

When he challenges his wife about her gifts, though, she always smiles and explains, "If it wasn't valuable, it wouldn't matter so much, would it? It has to be something I love before giving it away can be a statement of devotion to God . . . and a reminder to me of where my heart belongs."

Excellent point.

All of us (even those in vocational ministry) are subject to the "creeping entitlement" of our culture. We get a little from God, and, at first, we're thankful for the gift, but soon we see it as our sovereign right to have it. I know the trap from personal experience. That's what happened to me.

Years ago when I was a young evangelist, God blessed my ministry. The first week after God delivered me from my alcohol addiction, our church youth pastor wisely arranged for me to give my testimony in public. As a result of my message, a number of kids from my high school, who had come to see the spectacle of my preaching, accepted Christ. In fact, four of them were baptized along with me later that same night—I was baptized along with my first four converts! But the power of accountability kicked in. I was "on the hook" for Jesus.

> A peace treaty with an idol always leaves the idol in charge.

Within weeks, I was traveling our area preaching revivals, and it never quit. My opportunities for ministry only grew. By the time I was twenty, I was looking pretty good—at least to myself—on the evangelism circuit. I had been raised in humble circumstances, and suddenly I was running in circles with a number of famous Christian leaders. It was intoxicating!

To keep up an appropriate appearance, I bought designer suits, name-brand shoes, and top-dollar shirts. I even carried a Montblanc pen. "I've suffered so much in my life," I rationalized, "and I've done so much good for God, I deserve all this." I was dead wrong, of course (although I would never have admitted it). If anyone had confronted me by pointing out my sense of entitlement, I would have been deeply offended and denied it. My heart was blind to the idols that were creeping onto its altar.

God let me drift in this wonderland of deception for a long time, and that's when God's call came for me to move from my position of growing national acclaim to the small town pastorate in Arkansas. I had to confront the fixations of my heart. The trappings of wealth and success had become an idol to me, and idols don't die quietly. We have to grab them by the throat and kill them without mercy. During the process, we'll come up with a thousand reasons why we should keep on living the same way, or worse, we'll make only a partial commitment to change. A peace treaty with an idol always leaves the idol in charge. No, it has to die. The idol must be totally vanquished. Nothing short of complete destruction of the false gods will free us from the grip of idolatry.

In the course of wrestling with God, trying to compromise with my idols, weeping and praying, God showed me that my recognition and success had become more important than He. If you had asked me about it the day before the fateful cell phone call from the Arkansas church wanting me to become their pastor, I would have laughed at the idea of idolatry in my life. But God's Spirit wouldn't let me go on lying to Him and to me. Gradually, I realized I must slay the beast and put God back on the throne of my heart. It was one of the most excruciating—yet liberating— experiences of my life. And I have to do it again and again to keep my heart pure. Now, though, I'm not surprised when God shines the light of truth and conviction on something that has become too precious to me. I've been there before, and I know what I have to do. It's still not easy, but at least I have a track record.

This struggle with good-things-becoming-idols is not new to our culture. People have faced the same temptation in various forms for centuries. The story of Abraham and Isaac happened in a far different culture nearly four thousand years ago, but the message is as fresh as this morning's first cup of coffee.

Abraham and Sarah had waited twenty-five years for God to fulfill His promise to give them a son. It's hard to imagine the ecstasy they felt when at last they cradled a child in their arms. Their gratitude to the God who gave them such a precious gift seemed beyond measure. Yet within a dozen years or so, the old man's affections had shifted from the Giver to the gift, from God to Isaac, from the Maker to Abraham's son. In one of the most heart-wrenching commands in the Bible, God directs Abraham to kill Isaac as a sacrifice to the Almighty. Surely Abraham's heart was torn to pieces, but he chose to obey. The old father and his son traveled three days to Mount Moriah, and after building an altar, Abraham laid Isaac on the sacrificial platform and raised a knife over his son. At that moment, God knew—and more importantly, Abraham knew—that the patriarch's heart had come back home. If he was willing to slay his only son, the son of the promise, the old man's repentance was real.

In the same way, God doesn't dance around with half measures when an Isaac in our lives has supplanted him at the center of our hearts. It could be a child, a spouse, a dream, a career, an addiction, or something else, but God won't bargain with us about it. He demands that we put our misplaced desire (not an actual person) on the altar, pull out the knife, and kill it there. Nothing else will do.

When we make these dramatic decisions—and every believer is called to make them from time to time because our hearts drift toward our Isaacs and away from God—the moment is excruciating, but we find freedom, joy, and peace like we haven't known in a long time, or maybe ever. We no longer worry about protecting our Isaac. Nothing matters more than being right with God. Paradoxically, when God is at the center, we can enjoy our lives and the people we love far more than before—and even they know it. Before the extravagant act of obedience on Mount Moriah, Abraham's relationship with Isaac was tainted by the idolatry of valuing his son above God. That day, however, removed the poison. Then, father and son could relish their relationship under the smile of God.

People often misunderstand what it means to surrender everything to God. They think God wants to take away all we value and ruin our lives, but reality is exactly the opposite. God wants us to give Him everything and put Him first so we can *truly enjoy* the gifts He gives us. We can only experience freedom and the limitless blessings of God if we put Him first.

Has security, a pursuit, or a person become an Isaac to you? Listen to God, and don't pay attention to the whines and bargaining of misplaced desires. Slay the disordered love, and put your supreme affection back where it belongs. You'll love better and live better with God in the center of your heart.

Think Outside the Box

139

1. *Are there sinful things in your life that stand between you and God right now? How about things that aren't necessarily sinful but just in the way? What do you need to do to change that?*
2. *Is there something in your life that you've come to feel entitled to—but you're not really?*
3. *Re-read Jeremiah 2:23-24. I raise the question of whether or not Jeremiah is being too harsh on the people of Israel. What do you think?*
4. *How have you seen God's best outshine what you thought was good?*
5. *Is there an Isaac in your life? What act of extravagant devotion do you need to take in order to put it back in its proper place?*

chapter 13

work of the Spirit

One of the most fascinating and important principles of spiritual life is that God artfully connects two realms: the eternal and the temporal, the infinite and the finite, the spiritual and the physical, the unseen and the seen, the intangible and the tangible. The Old Testament tabernacle—and later the temple—was the place where heaven and earth intersected. In the New Testament, Paul carries forward the theme by explaining that our bodies are the "temple of the Holy Spirit." We don't have to go to a temple or a church to experience the presence of the holy, awesome, infinite God. He lives inside us!

Partners

As I pointed out in Chapter 2, Scripture recounts that Jesus offered people the incredible privilege of participating with Him in His work. And in fact, the principle remains that He often withholds His miraculous powers until we do our part to put the wheels of blessing in motion. In C. S. Lewis' essay, "The Efficacy of Prayer," he comments on God's willingness to partner with us:

> *For He seems to do nothing of Himself which He can possibly delegate to His creatures. He commands us to do slowly and blunderingly what He could do perfectly and in the twinkling of an eye. He allows us to neglect what He would have us do, or to fail. Perhaps we do not fully*

realize the problem, so to call it, of enabling finite free wills to co-exist with Omnipotence. It seems to involve at every moment almost a sort of divine abdication. We are not mere recipients or spectators. We are either privileged to share in the game or compelled to collaborate in the work, "to wield our little tridents." Is this amazing process simply Creation going on before our eyes? This is how (no light matter) God makes something . . . out of nothing. [32]

At the pinnacle of His ministry, crowds of people flocked to Jesus because they wanted to be healed, or at least to see others healed. Imagine how His miracles would be covered on CNN! At one point on a dusty hill, 5,000 men (probably 20,000 people including women and children) sat to hear Him teach and see Him perform miracles. Knowing the people would be getting hungry after a day's worth of taking in His teaching, Jesus turned to Philip and asked, "Where shall we buy bread for these people to eat?" (John 6:5). Jesus was testing the disciple to see if he had the vision to trust Jesus to miraculously feed the throngs, but poor Philip didn't have a clue. Jesus intentionally had brought him and the rest of the disciples to a pivotal point of need. John tells us Jesus "already had in mind what he was going to do" (John 6:6).

This story is shared in all four gospels, and each time the writer makes sure to report specific figures so we understand the situation: there were 5,000 men, five loaves of bread, and two fish in the boy's lunch, and after the meal, twelve baskets of leftovers. Although the people were hungry, we can assume they weren't starving. A healthy human

---

32. C. S. Lewis, "The Efficacy of Prayer," from *The World's Last Night and Other Essays*, 378–392.

body can survive for several weeks with little or no food. The point of the story wasn't that the people were desperate for food. They would have lived whether Jesus had fed them or not. The message that day wasn't about the masses. It was about the disciples.

Jesus invited his closest followers to join Him in a miracle. He asked Philip for advice, and He accepted Andrew's offer of the boy's lunch. At least Andrew was on the right track. His offer is absurd in a purely physical sense. What good could a single sack of food do for a stadium full of people? But Jesus was thrilled that the disciple brought up a tangible resource. To that "offering," Jesus added His intangible might to multiply the food for the crowd. Even then, He directed His men to partner in the miracle by distributing the food and picking up baskets of leftovers.

> Jesus invited His closest followers to join Him in a miracle.

143

If Jesus had performed it all by Himself—which He certainly could have done—the disciples would have been observers instead of partners. Jesus knew there would come a day when the privilege and responsibility of feeding the souls of the world would rest on their shoulders. The disciples needed to understand that their role was crucial to the success of God's venture—on the hillside that day, and later across the planet as they took the gospel to every tribe, tongue, and nation.

Building Your Faith Memory

Some leaders in the church today teach that if we walk with Jesus, we'll never experience darkness or need, but that's simply not true. The Lord leads us into light, but sooner or later, the God of light takes us to dark places where our only option is to trust Him. Jesus tested the disciples that day to see if they had enough faith and creativity to feed the crowd, and He tests us in similar ways.

Every decision point tests our faith, and every success lodges in our faith's memory banks to strengthen us for the next test. If we're not careful, though, we sometimes fail to learn the lessons of faith from past experiences (like Jehovah Jireh's provision through a year without a paycheck). After the stunning miracle on the hill that day, Jesus sent His men in a boat across the lake. During the night, a fierce storm blew up. As they strained to row the boat, they saw Jesus walking on the water. They were terrified, but Jesus got into the boat with them, and the storm subsided. Only hours before, they had witnessed Jesus performing a miracle, but it hadn't penetrated their souls. In Mark's account, he says, "They were completely amazed, for they had not understood about the loaves; their hearts were hardened" (Mark 6:51-52).

> We need to marvel at God's amazing power.

144

We can be right in the middle of the greatest movement of God in our lifetime but fail to grasp it. There have been times I've been frustrated by people who seem oblivious to the fact that Almighty God had just performed a glorious miracle among them, yet quickly lost faith. But the Lord soon reminded me, "They're no different from the disciples, and, Bryan, they're no different from you a lot of the time." (Like when I had to give up my house to learn the lesson—again!) To be full partners with God, we must open our eyes to the wedding of tangible and intangible. We need to marvel at God's amazing power, and let the God events we are part of sink deep into our hearts so they encourage our faith for the next step, the next trapeze, in our adventure with Him.

A worthwhile side note to the story of Jesus' feeding the 5,000: the common people got the message better than the disciples. In response to the miracle of the multiplied lunch, they believed Jesus and chased after Him. When they realized the next morning that He had left, they ran around to the other side of the sea to find Him. On their way, they told everybody in the region about what Jesus had done. (*That's* a sign of a true spiritual awakening!) Mark describes the scene:

> When {Jesus and the disciples} had crossed over, they landed at Gennesaret and anchored there. As soon as they got out of the boat, people recognized Jesus. They ran throughout that whole region and carried the sick on mats to wherever they heard he was. And wherever he went —into villages, towns or countryside—they placed the sick in the marketplaces. They begged him to let them touch even the edge of his cloak, and all who touched him were healed. (*Mark 6:53-56*)

Jesus had used the supernatural provision of a simple meal to convince people He could give them something much more important: eternal life.

A Family Gift

Seeing God take our small but tangible offerings and do magnificent miracles with what we present Him is one of the most exciting parts of the Christian life. Although I'm a slow learner, I'm actually starting to enjoy the rigorous training God requires of those who have made themselves a living sacrifice.

Two years after our Dallas church paid off its debt, we had outgrown our church facilities, and our church held another campaign to expand. As the leader of our church, I realized my responsibility to be a model of generosity for the church family. My pockets, though, were empty. I had given up my salary for a year. Then we had given away our home and every dime we had. I wanted to be an example of complete trust, uncommon obedience, courageous faith, and outrageous generosity, but I had nothing to give.

> "What's in your hand?" (Exodus 4:2)

I asked God, "Lord, what do you want me to do?"

The Lord reminded me of what He asked Moses through the burning bush: "What's in your hand?" (Exodus 4:2).

Although I didn't have money or equity in a home to give away, I immediately realized I had the talents with which He had entrusted me. I had the ability to communicate, a passion for the message God had put on my heart, and a network of relationships with church leaders across the country. That was something I could use for God in a new way. I went to my board and told them I wanted to fulfill my financial pledge by traveling to speak at churches around the nation. I could give "sweat equity" by turning over all my honorariums to the church. The board approved my "second job," and Haley and I pledged $150,000 to the new building fund.

To kick off the capital campaign, our church rented the Eisemann Performing Arts Center. People poured in for the landmark event, many of them anxious to present their well-thought-out pledges to the church's need. When my then four-year-old daughter, Addisyn, walked into the Eisemann Center that Sunday, an usher who didn't realize she was my daughter greeted her. In keeping with the spirit of the morning, he asked, "And what are you bringing to give to the Lord this morning?"

Without a pause, she looked at him and answered, "My daddy."

She was right. My commitment that day required an immense sacrifice by everyone in my family. I had promised the church board that my travels would not undermine my service to our church. Nearly every week for two years, I slipped out of the last morning service to a car waiting to speed me to the airport. I would catch an afternoon flight to wherever I needed to be for an evening service as guest preacher. Sometime between the time that service would end and first thing Monday morning, I would fly home, arriving in time for my church staff meeting to start the week.

All my travels required a lot of Haley and the children. Not only did they give up my presence at home for a hundred Sundays, they sometimes had to put up with an over-extended, exhausted preacher when I did spend time at home. So Addisyn was dead on. I had given what was "in my hand" to offer God, and the family had given what they had—me. They gave me to the churches where I preached, and they gave me to our church where the money has been donated. Every member of our family has given generously and gladly to the Lord.

Even though I worked hard to make good on my pledge, God still rewarded my family and me with a chance to see Him finalize the deal on His terms, with a profound miracle. He worked out many things along the way, but I must tell you how He was the One who multiplied what I offered.

With just over a month remaining of my two-year commitment to give speaking honorariums to the church, Haley and I had donated $130,000 of the $150,000 we had pledged. But suddenly, the invitations to speak dried up. I had nothing else on my calendar that would bring in more money. We considered trying to feel okay that perhaps the amount we'd given was "good enough," but neither of us was at peace with the thought.

Two weeks later, no more money and no more speaking engagements had come my way, and I was feeling pretty discouraged. So much so that one afternoon when my assistant passed along a message that an old friend was trying to get in touch with me, I decided to ignore the call. It had been years since I'd spoken with this guy, and I was sure we had little in common at that point. After considerable internal debate, however, I finally relented, called the long-lost acquaintance and agreed to meet him for coffee. Apparently, he was just passing through town and wanted to see me.

At our meeting, I was pleasantly surprised to learn that he had been following my ministry for several years and listened regularly to my podcasts. That was gratifying, of course, but it in no way prepared me for what God did next through the faithful servant sitting across the table from me.

"Bryan, I have something for you, but before I give it to you, I must tell you a condition that comes with it. When I was growing up, my parents were in ministry, and I saw them repeatedly give everything they had to the church. I have a gift for you, but I want you to promise that you'll use it for whatever you and Haley want, not your ministry."

With that, he laid on the table a check for $20,000. I just stared at it.

When I found words, I told him my condition for accepting the gift. "If it's really for Haley and me to do with *whatever* we want, then I must warn that you may be disappointed."

As I explained the miracle in which he was playing a part, he was pleased to let me add his check to the $130,000 I had already given to the church. Haley and I made our pledge, with a few days to spare.

Of course, I wasn't the only person in our church who offered something to God that He multiplied. Some took on actual second jobs to have funds to give. A few started businesses they'd been thinking about, and as God prospered, they donated their profits to the church. We even saw older folks come out of retirement just so they could participate in the giving.

After the Sunday Addisyn gave me to the church, God has worked in the life of our congregation in astounding ways. People have given more than ever, found the love to reach out to family, friends, and neighbors, and shared the grace of Jesus with people throughout our community. That's what God intends when He asks us to use what we have available. Our tangible donations to His cause return intangible rewards we could never have imagined.

Think Outside the Box

1. *In the feeding of the 5,000, what was the role of the disciples? What was Jesus' role? Why was it important for the disciples to play an active role in the miracle?*
2. *Can you think of a time when you missed a moment of opportunity to participate in a miracle? What caused you to miss it? Fear? Doubt? The desire for comfort or approval? How has this failure prepared you to take advantage of the next opportunity in your life?*
3. *What experiences have helped build your faith memory?*
4. *Consider the story about raising $150,000 through a second job. Have you ever been tempted to stop short in a commitment you've made to God because you didn't see how He would come through for you? If you "kept the faith," what happened? How did that help your faith memory?*
5. *What does "intangible reward" mean to you?*

chapter 14

go and do likewise?

Should you give up your salary for a year? Deed your house over to your church? How about take on a second job so you can increase your charitable giving?

I seriously doubt that God will direct you to do the exact same things He's required of me. His plan for each of us is tuned to our individual needs for spiritual growth. He has no one-size-fits-all plan for His people.

If you forsake your salary for a year, you and your family might starve. If you give your home away, you might end up living under a bridge. If you take on another job just because I did or do something else God hasn't specifically led you to do, He won't bless. You'll suffer needlessly, and you'll blame God (maybe me, too) for the resulting disaster. It's not the specifics of my story that are important, but the underlying principles of extravagant devotion, surrender, and obedience. God asks these things from each of us. So lest you decide to do one of the same crazy things I've done, let's review a few principles you can apply to help you discern what God might be asking of you.

Connect the Tangible to the Intangible

We operate in the physical world, but God is far bigger than that. If we devote what we can see, touch, smell, and taste to the Lord, He will open the gates of heaven to bless us—spiritually, physically, financially, and every other way.

Don't Expect a Perfectly Pure Response to God's Leading

If you get nothing else out of my story, realize that I fought *against* God's instructions long and hard before I found the courage to do what God had clearly led me to do. Mine was anything but instant and complete obedience, but, praise God, I eventually found the courage to say "yes" to Him. Don't be surprised if you're assailed by doubts, questions, and hesitations of every kind. Work through them, seek the counsel of godly people who have a proven track record of radical obedience (all the others will think you're crazy!), and look for God's confirmation through Scripture, circumstances, and the Spirit's nudging.

> Extravagant devotion is the normal response of a heart open to the wondrous grace of Jesus.

152

Realize That Radical Obedience Isn't Optional

There aren't first-class and second-class Christians, an A Team and a B Team. Jesus calls all of us to deny our selfishness, take up the cross of sacrificial obedience, and grab His hand to follow wherever He leads. One mark of true faith is our willingness to give, love, and serve, expecting nothing in return. Extravagant devotion isn't for super-Christians, and it's not relegated to particular times in our lives. It's the normal response of a heart open to the wondrous grace of Jesus. On the other hand, not every moment in the Christian life is a call to radical sacrifice and suffering. We enjoy many times of peace and blessing. I've found myself in times of relative tranquility in my walk with Jesus that can even feel a bit like walking in darkness. Sometimes the more exciting periods make us feel more alive in Him, but times of greater adventure don't stay with us forever.

If you can't identify a number of times, though, when God has called you to uncomfortable, challenging risks of faith, you have reason to wonder if you understand what it truly means to be His child.

Take First Steps First

God probably won't require you to give *everything* until you've faithfully given *something*. The first step for many of us is to carve out a regular time to read the Bible and pray every day, to turn off the television and talk to our families, to take the risk my mother took to trust God to bless the 90 percent more than the tightly held 100 percent, to sign up for a project to help people in the community, or to go on a mission trip. The options are almost endless. Ask God to lead you. Make yourself available, and you can be sure He'll take you up on your offer.

153

It's Not All About Money

Some Christians get upset anytime a pastor or church leader talks about money. By contrast, I've noticed that unbelievers and new believers typically don't have any problem with talk about finances. They accept that funding any organization requires money. The ones who resist pastors talking about money, tithing, personal debt, and church budgets are likely the ones walking out of the will of God, those who haven't surrendered their hearts to the Lord. They sometimes complain to me, "Pastor, I wish you wouldn't talk so much about money. It makes me feel uncomfortable."

People who live in extravagant devotion to God know that everything they have is God's, and they want to use every dollar, minute, and talent to honor Him. They aren't offended when the pastor talks about money. Rather, they want input to know how to use money wisely for God's kingdom.

The reason extravagance is not all about money, however, is that money remains simply a tangible expression of what we truly value. When we have it in our bank accounts, we have complete autonomy to make any decision about it. If we believe possessions and pleasures are essential to our identity, we'll hoard money or spend it wastefully. But if our identities are wrapped up in God, we'll want every dollar to honor Him.

Live So That You Won't Have Regrets

I don't want to look back years from now and wish I'd pushed all my chips to the center of the table in my walk with God. I don't want to grow old and be haunted by a lot of "what ifs" and "if onlys." The choices I make today determine tomorrow's memories. God gives me only a certain number of days, dollars, and talents. I want to invest all of them for God and His kingdom so I'll have grateful memories and few regrets.

154

As you take steps to give, love, and serve, God will bless, and you'll get excited about giving—whatever it is—even more. Soon, you'll want to dip into the 90 percent to fund the Kingdom, and you'll want to give more time to help needy people or reach the unreached. Before long, your hearts will be so full of God's amazing grace that you give like David's donation to construct the temple, Solomon's offering of 142,000 animals to sacrifice at the dedication of the temple, Mary's alabaster jar of expensive perfume poured on Jesus' feet, and the widow's two mites. This kind of giving is never forced. It flows out of a heart full of gratitude.

While most of us devote our lives to self-protection, avoiding risks at all costs and valuing comfort and affluence above all else, this lifestyle is the opposite of biblical Christianity. God always asks for our whole heart. And sometimes, He asks for at least some of the things that have crept into the center of our affections so He can purge us from these idols. It's the way of the cross. Don't miss the power of this truth, or your spiritual life will always be shallow and weak. You may not be called to give exactly the way I have, but you *will be called* to your own version of extravagant devotion.

Think Outside the Box

1. *"I seriously doubt that God will direct you to do the exact same things He's required of me." Why?*
2. *What connections have you observed between the tangible and the intangible?*
3. *What obstacles and objections do you need to work through right now in order to respond to God with a wholehearted "Yes"?*
4. *What makes extravagant devotion a "normal response" to God?*
5. *Since God won't require you to give everything until you've given something, what is the something you need to give first?*
6. *Are you uncomfortable with "spiritual" talk about money? If so, why?*
7. *Are you on a path of living with or without regrets?*

155

15

the most extravagant gift of all

In countless conversations with people over the years, I've noticed a singular truth: the quality of their most cherished relationships produces the highest joys and the deepest pains. I've talked to adults who told me with glad tears in their eyes about the love their moms and dads had shown them. And I've seen the pain etched on the faces of people who felt abused or abandoned by family members. Relationships with parents, spouses, and children make our lives rich and meaningful, or they create deep, searing wounds. "Rich and meaningful" can simply be enjoyed as part of life, but usually "deep, searing wounds" require healing and help to find their purpose. That's where perhaps the most difficult arena of extravagant devotion comes in.

A life of extravagant devotion to Christ means participating in the thing He demonstrated most clearly and values most dearly: forgiveness. Christian psychologist Archibald Hart explains, "Forgiveness is surrendering my right to hurt you for hurting me."[33]

In our churches, we talk a lot about forgiveness, but sadly, we aren't very good at it. Because we don't forgive, most of us live with a degree of bitterness, simmering disappointment, barely contained rage, or a nagging sense of estrangement. It doesn't have to be this way. Extravagance

---

33. Archibald Hart, *Thrilled to Death*, (Nashville: Thomas Nelson Publishers, 2007), 248.

for God always involves learning to give and receive the gift of forgiveness. In fact, the *most extravagant* thing a person can do is forgive someone who doesn't deserve it. That's the awesome nature of God's grace toward us.

His Forgiveness in You

> The most extravagant thing a person can do is forgive someone who doesn't deserve it.

There's no way we can do this in our own power, but fortunately it's not up to us to "dig deep" and manufacture forgiving behaviors. God produces them from the inside out as we focus on His grace and surrender to Him. The Christian life isn't a "grit your teeth" endurance contest. If we look to God, He supernaturally makes us more like Christ. As we grow more devoted to Him, we tap into His heart. Then His love and power flow through us by the power of the Holy Spirit. We can't overflow, though, if our well isn't full.

We can only love the unlovely, forgive offenders, and accept difficult people if God has worked the necessary character traits into our souls and filled our well to overflowing. Three Scripture passages explain:

- "This is love: not that we loved God, but that He loved us and sent his Son as an atoning sacrifice for our sins. Dear friends, since God so loved us, we also ought to love one another" (1 John 4:10-11). The apostle John, "the disciple Jesus loved" (John 20:21), felt Christ's love so overwhelmingly it shaped his whole identity. We know Jesus loved the other disciples, too, but John felt His love so deeply it spilled into his writing as he explained why we should love others.

- "Bear with each other and forgive whatever grievances you may have against one another. Forgive as the Lord forgave you" (Colossians 3:13). Paul gives believers in Colossae the same direction as John.
- "Accept one another, then, just as Christ accepted you, in order to bring praise to God" (Romans 15:7). Paul repeats the same message in another way to the Romans.

So we can love, forgive, and accept others to the extent—and only to the extent—that we have genuinely experienced the love, forgiveness, and acceptance of Christ for us.

Some Christians have the wrong idea about spiritual maturity. They think there should come a point when they no longer struggle with "the lust of the eyes, the lust of the flesh, and the boastful pride of life" (1 John 2:16), and they're right. That day will come. It's called heaven. While we're in this world, though, all of us will struggle with the old nature—and that includes the struggle to forgive. If we try to convince people around us that we've "arrived," we're being dishonest, and we're putting on masks instead of being authentic.

I believe we're all ordinary people who sometimes endure extraordinary pain. Yet God often reveals Himself most gloriously through our pain. God could have revealed Himself in any way He wanted, but He chose the language of pain, demonstrated most profoundly in Christ Himself. Jesus suffered and died a horrible death to connect with us at the most vulnerable points in our lives. He showed His extravagant love for us by enduring public ridicule, mock trials and conviction, excruciating whipping, and the most torturous death any government has ever devised. He endured incomprehensible physical suffering, but His spiritual pain was even worse. For the first time in all eternity, the Son was cut off from the Father specifically so He could bear our sins. He was forsaken so we could be embraced. As He hung on the cross bearing our sin and its consequences, He cried out, "My God, My God. Why have You forsaken Me?" (Matthew 27:46). Why did He bear such suffering? Not because He deserved it, but because we deserve it. He took our place, paying our price, and suffering the death we deserve. So we could be forgiven.

The love of God is strong enough to convince us we don't have to hide any longer. We can be honest with Him about our sin because He's already proven the depth of His love, even for sinners like us. And in His family, we can be honest with each other about our sins and hurts. We are wounded in relationships, yet we also experience God's healing in relationships—if we'll be real with one another.

When we're filled with His love, power, and forgiveness, the qualities of His grace flow into the broken lives of people around us. This isn't ordinary love. When we learn to love like Jesus, we don't just overlook every sin and defect in people's lives. We care enough to speak the truth—not to condemn but to offer a path of change. The love of Jesus isn't codependent and weak. It's strong, vibrant, and full of truth, and it always looks for a way to help people change and grow. Relating to an addict or an abuser, for instance, requires "tough love," like my mom showed me when she discovered my drinking problem. To love that way, we need a large measure of God's wisdom and strength.

The Source of a Forgiving Heart

One of the most amazing things people found in the life of Jesus is that He was willing to forgive anyone who was willing to reach out for it. He forgave prostitutes, the hated tax collector Zacchaeus, an outcast Samaritan woman, and even those who nailed Him to the cross. His forgiveness knew no limits.

The disciples, I'm sure, were astounded to see Him go far beyond the normal teachings about human relationships. Jewish law had long before tried to curb the escalation of retaliation by instituting *lex talionis*, "an eye for an eye and a tooth for a tooth." Jesus, though, said equal retaliation wasn't appropriate for those who are in God's kingdom. We need to go farther, to forgive those who have offended us.

> The love of God is strong enough to convince us we don't have to hide any longer.

One day, Peter tried to get his mind around this extra-mile forgiveness idea and asked, "Lord, how many times shall I forgive my brother when he sins against me? Up to seven times?" (Matthew 18:21). Peter must have thought seven sounded fairly honorable, but Jesus must have squelched a laugh when He replied, "I tell you, not seven times, but seventy-seven times." His comment was hyperbole, but Jesus was making the point that there are no limits to our forgiveness, just as there are no limits on God's forgiveness of us. To show what forgiveness looks like in practice, He told Peter and the others a parable about two servants in a king's court. The first servant owed the king the astronomical debt of ten thousand talents. Some Bible scholars have noted that this amount of money was equal to the gross domestic product of the three surrounding nations! The amount was so incredibly large that it was impossible to repay. Perhaps the servant was a high-ranking government official in charge of the kingdom's treasury, and he had squandered the money in scandalous dealings.

Some suggest that's the only way such a huge debt could be incurred.

When the servant was brought before the king and re-payment was demanded, he didn't have the money, of course. The king ordered him to be thrown into debtors' prison, but he pleaded for time to repay the debt. Even though he'd still be there today trying to pay it off, the king had mercy and completely forgave him. The man had walked into the king's palace with an incredible debt, no hope to repay it, and a lifetime of prison in his future. He walked out completely free!

> Those who appreciate the depth of God's forgiveness become good forgivers.

As he walked away from the palace, though, the servant saw a colleague who owed him a few dollars. He not only demanded to be repaid, he grabbed him and choked him! The man pleaded for time to pay back what he owed, but the first servant refused. He ordered that the man be thrown into debtors' prison until he repaid the full amount.

Other servants of the king observed both scenes, in the palace and on the street, and they informed their master. Outraged, the king called the first servant back to the palace. "You wicked servant," he growled, "I canceled all that debt of yours because you begged me to. Shouldn't you have had mercy on your fellow servant just as I had on you?" (Matthew 18:32-33). The king turned him over "to be tortured" until he paid back the full amount of his original debt. At the end of the parable, Jesus utters one of the most piercing statements in the Bible: "This is how my heavenly Father will treat each of you unless you forgive your brother from your heart" (Matthew 18:35).

Wow! Jesus made it absolutely clear: We're like the first servant, owing a mountain of debt, needing a wealth of mercy, and holding a mass of responsibility. Even the best of us carries a mega-debt of sin to God our King. It's so huge there's not a shred of hope we could repay it. Our only hope is to fall on His mercy and grace and beg for His extravagant forgiveness. Those who truly appreciate the depth of God's forgiveness become good forgivers. But those who don't keep their hearts flooded by God's grace soon forget it. Then they act like the first servant. They refuse to forgive people and try to choke the life out of the offenders in every way they can.

God is not happy when we don't forgive as He forgives us. Luke 12:48 reminds us that "to whom much is given much is required." The first servant, like many of us, failed the test of responsibility. When we won't pass along the forgiveness God abundantly, extravagantly poured out on us, we suffer. He lets us be tortured by bitterness, regret and daydreams of revenge. This ruins every relationship in which we hold back forgiveness, and it blocks the flow of the Holy Spirit in everything we do. Refusing to forgive is one of the most immovable obstacles to a life of extravagant devotion. But learning to forgive helps us tap into the heart of God like nothing else on earth. This is a vital truth.

163

The Choice to Forgive

Do you find it hard to love, forgive, and accept people around you? From time to time, we all do, and to be sure, some of us live with exceptionally difficult people. We can't just grit our teeth and make ourselves respond to them with God's compassion and strength. It has to come from inside, from our own rich, deep, compelling experience of Christ's love for us. Author and pastor Lewis Smedes teaches that forgiveness is categorically different from merely excusing the person who hurt us. He explains:

When we forgive evil we do not excuse it, we do not tolerate it, we do not smother it. We look the evil full in the face, call it what it is, let its horror shock and stun and enrage us, and only then do we forgive it.[34]

The miracle of forgiveness starts when we acknowledge the evil that requires forgiveness and then forgive anyway.

I've had to choose to forgive two men who hurt me deeply—one who abandoned me and one who abused me. My father ran out on our family when I was a little boy, and another relative sexually abused me for several years, beginning when I was a boy and continuing into my pre-teen years. I harbored bitterness, unforgiveness, and even hatred toward both of them for many years, and the pain almost consumed me.

Like many kids in divorced homes, I took sides and blamed my father for all the family's problems. In adolescence, I suffered the shame of my relative's abuse even after it had ended. As I explained in my testimony, I used alcohol to numb the emotional pain and unrelenting shame. After I became a Christian, God began to work the miracle of grace into the recesses of my heart. In a radical conversion, He mercifully and abruptly freed me from the alcohol abuse and all that comes with it. The pain, though, didn't go away. Every time someone mentioned wounds, abuse, or men in authority, it was like throwing gasoline on a fire I'd hoped was already out. It wasn't. Any mention of those sensitive issues caused a fresh explosion of hurt, bitterness, and rage. I wanted to follow God with every ounce of my being, but I simply couldn't figure out how to deal with the pain of the past that haunted me.

164

34. Lewis Smedes, *Forgive and Forget*, (Harper & Row, 1984), 79-80.

As I grew closer to God, the light of His love exposed the deep-seated resentment I'd carried for so long, and I began to experience healing. Just before Haley and I were married, we heard a preacher talk about the conditions necessary for forgiveness. His sermon rattled me to the core. He shared several passages of Scripture which teach the message of Jesus' parable in Matthew 18. That is, if we refuse to forgive people who have hurt us, we won't experience the blessings of God's forgiving us. In the Sermon on the Mount, Jesus explained, "For if you forgive men when they sin

Because I'm forgiven, I must forgive.

against you, your heavenly Father will also forgive you. But if you do not forgive men their sins, your Father will not forgive your sins" (Matthew 6:14-15).

As I learned about the conditions of forgiveness, my perspective on my father and my abuser slowly changed. As Jesus' parable depicts, because I'm forgiven, I must forgive, or I'll experience the torture of bitterness. In his book, *The Parables*, Gary Inrig tells a story about how revenge is a destructive priority in some people's lives:

> *A man got bit by a dog that was later discovered to have rabies. The man was rushed to the hospital where tests showed that he, too, had contracted the highly contagious disease. At that time, medical science had not discovered a cure for rabies, so the doctor told the man he needed to get his affairs in order. The dying man sank back in his bed in shock for a few minutes, and then summoned the strength to ask for a pen and paper. When the doctor stopped by a bit later to check on him, he was writing with great*

165

energy. The doctor said, "Oh, good. I'm glad to see you are working on your will."

"This ain't no will," the man answered. "It's a list of all the people I'm going to bite before I die!"[35]

We hold on to bitterness because it gives us two things we want: identity and energy. We see ourselves as "the one who was wronged," so we feel justified in our self-pity, and thoughts of revenge give us a daily shot of adrenaline. But make no mistake: bitterness poisons the soul. For years, I lay awake in bed every night, secretly plotting to get even with the man who had abused me. I had no idea how thoroughly these thoughts were ruining me, but the target of my anger wasn't affected by them in the least. I was the only injured party in my thought life. In *Wishful Thinking*, Pastor Frederick Buechner observes:

> *Of the Seven Deadly Sins, anger is possibly the most fun. To lick your wounds, to smack your lips over grievances long past, to roll over your tongue the prospect of bitter confrontations still to come, to savor to the last toothsome morsel both the pain you are given and the pain you are giving back—in many ways it is a feast fit for a king. The chief drawback is that what you are wolfing down is yourself. The skeleton at the feast is you!*[36]

God's Spirit worked on me just as surely as I worked on the problem of revenge. The more of Christ's grace I enjoyed, the more I wanted to "clear up past accounts." Although neither

---

35. Gary Inrig, *The Parables* (Grand Rapids: Discovery House, 1991), 63.
36. Frederick Buechner, *Wishful Thinking* (San Francisco: Harper Collins, 1993), 2.

of the people who had hurt me most ever confessed their sins or asked for forgiveness, I realized God had commanded me to forgive them whether they ever asked for it or not, whether they changed or not, or whether they responded with true repentance or not. As the love, forgiveness, and acceptance of Christ sank deep into my soul, I went to my relative's office and told him, "I don't expect you to respond, but I want you to know that I forgive you."

My forgiveness didn't change him, but it did change me. I no longer staggered around under the burden of resentment. Although I still grieved the wounds, I chose not to take revenge in any way—inwardly by delighting in bad things that happened to him or outwardly by gossiping about him. The medicine of forgiveness gradually healed the wounds of that part of my past, but it wasn't my only forgiveness hurdle.

> My forgiveness didn't change him, but it did change me.

While I was in seminary, I flew to Illinois to preach at a revival. My father, who had been sick for some time and waiting for a heart transplant, lived in nearby St. Louis. When Haley and I arrived at the airport, to my shock, my father picked us up. Unbeknownst to me, he attended the church at which I was to preach. In the car, things were, to say the least, a bit awkward. He invited us to stay at his house, though, and as we were taking our luggage inside, my father stopped in the doorway, turned to me, and said, "Son, I can't go back and undo the past. I haven't done everything right, but God has forgiven me, and all I can ask is that you do the same."

I nodded my acceptance of his appeal, and at that moment restoration of our relationship took root. Reconciliation doesn't happen in an instant. It takes time to rebuild broken trust and establish lines of communication, but experiencing that is a glorious relief. I highly recommend it.

Allowing Forgiveness to Work

When we choose to forgive someone, we shouldn't expect all our hurt and anger to instantly subside. The wound is often too deep for that, and the processing of emotions requires patience. Even today, stabbing pain from the past can resurface in my life. When I think of someone sexually abusing one of my children, for example, fear and rage explode in my heart, and I have to think and pray myself down from the ledge. Emotions can be wild and fickle, not tame animals we can easily command. Gradually, the powerful reactions to our wounds give way to peace, but they never completely go away. While we always live with a scar, remember that a scar results from healing.

> True forgiveness starts with brutal honesty.

People often make one of two mistakes when they face the need to forgive someone who hurt them: they either make mountains out of molehills, or they make molehills out of mountains. Some of us are so brittle that we're crushed by even the slightest perception of an offense. If someone looks at us the wrong way, we feel like we've been stabbed in the heart. Sometimes, though, we've simply misunderstood the person, and sometimes the person misunderstood what we said or did. Before we put anyone in the category of "Personal Enemy Number One," we need to do a little investigation and ask a few questions. What we thought was a terrible offense may not have been a big deal after all.

The other error is just as common. Many of us don't want to face the hard reality that a person we loved and trusted has betrayed us. Instead of being honest about the traumatic situation and our pain, we minimize what happened ("oh, it wasn't that bad"), we excuse it ("she couldn't help it"), or we deny the event even occurred ("I don't even know what you're talking about"). Minimizing, excusing, and denying, however, *prevent* us from forgiving. People who have suffered prolonged abuse or abandonment often have the biggest problem being honest about the reality of their pain and the person's sin that caused it. They haven't ever seen honesty and forgiveness modeled, and they don't have much hope that God or anyone else can heal their pain. Without hope and skills, they remain stuck in the swamp of bitterness and blame-shifting, always pinning the fault on others and never facing their need for healing.

True forgiveness starts with brutal honesty. Quite often, it takes a friend to help begin the journey. Sooner or later, we'll be able to separate the excusable from the inexcusable, and with a heart full of God's great grace, we'll be able to forgive the indefensible wrongs even as Jesus has forgiven the same in us.

Forgiveness almost always requires the forgiver to go through the process of grieving. Wounds don't heal immediately. They take time, attention, and the salve of the Holy Spirit. I had repressed my hurt and anger about my dad for many years. When he asked me to forgive him, I had the choice to continue suppressing the pain or let it surface so I could deal with it. I chose the more difficult, healing path. Over time, my father and I developed a good and honest relationship, and it was intensely rewarding. About the time he received his new physical heart and recovered from the surgery, he asked God for a new spiritual heart. He was wonderfully converted!

When I chose to forgive my father, both of us were liberated. I was freed from the bondage of bitterness, and he escaped the prison of shame. Forgiveness is the key that unlocks the ball and chain.

When you're damaged, the person who hurt you is like the lock on your life. If you refuse to forgive, you drag that person into your marriage, your relationship with your kids, every friendship, and to work with you every day. He may be a thousand miles away, or she may be dead, but unforgiveness keeps you attached to that person until you find the courage to turn the key and release yourself. Only then can you offer a relationship based on trust and respect. True reconciliation is built over time, and if the person accepts, you can take small steps of trust to see what happens. It's important along the way to avoid the ditches on either side of the road: being naïve and trusting too quickly or having a hard heart and refusing to trust even when the person proves trustworthy. God's wisdom is necessary to keep you on the road, and often that comes through good and godly input from a wise friend or two.

Forgiveness and Trust

There's a big difference between forgiveness and trust. Many people refuse to forgive because they don't want to trust someone who is untrustworthy, but the fact is, God doesn't want us to have faith in people who haven't proven to be trustworthy. That would be foolish. We are commanded to forgive, but we aren't commanded to trust other people. I forgave both my father and the man who abused me, but my relationship with them later became quite different. My father proved himself a changed man, and he earned my trust. But my other relative has never admitted his sin, and he refuses to talk with me about it. I have forgiven him, but I certainly don't trust him. I wouldn't allow my children to spend time with him.

We are commanded by God to forgive no matter how horribly the person treated us, and even when he or she is not sorry, is unrepentant, and doesn't seem to care. We forgive to resolve the hurt and anger *in us* and to express the forgiveness we've experienced *from God*. But trust can't be just one way; it takes both parties earning each other's trust through consistently honorable actions over time. It's entirely possible—and in some cases, necessary—to forgive someone but not trust him. No one said it's easy to forgive and offer to rebuild a relationship, but when reconciliation happens, it's a magnificent demonstration of extravagant devotion to God and the courage to take hard steps of faith.

There's a big difference between forgiveness and trust.

Our refusal to forgive keeps us locked in the prison of resentment. There are many reasons people refuse to forgive those who hurt them, including:

- He isn't sorry for what he did.
- She'll just do it again, so why bother.
- It wasn't an accident. He meant it!
- She's done it a lot of times.
- It was so horrible; how can I forgive something like that?
- I can't forgive because I'm still so hurt and angry. I'd be a hypocrite.
- It just doesn't make sense to let the offender off the hook.
- If I forgive, the person won't be brought to justice.

It's a challenge to forgive. Philip Yancey calls forgiving offenders "the unnatural act" because it flies in the face of our desire for revenge.[37] Similarly, C. S. Lewis observes candidly, "Forgiveness is a beautiful word, until you have something to forgive."[38]

When we forgive, we're not letting the person off the hook. We're merely transferring him or her from our hook to God's. Paul wrote:

> **We need to stop playing judge, and let Almighty God be the Judge.**

Do not repay anyone evil for evil. Be careful to do what is right in the eyes of everybody. If it is possible, as far as it depends on you, live at peace with everyone. Do not take revenge, my friends, but leave room for God's wrath, for it is written: It is mine to avenge; I will repay, says the Lord. (Romans 12:17-19)

172

We need to stop playing judge and let Almighty God be the Judge for whoever has hurt us. He has far greater wisdom and infinitely more resources to exact vengeance on the people who have caused us pain. When we put them in His mighty hands, we just might have reason to start feeling sorry for them!

---

37. Philip Yancey, *What's So Amazing about Grace?*, (Grand Rapids: Zondervan, 2002), 83-94.
38. C.S. Lewis, quoted in Robert Jeffress, *When Forgiveness Doesn't Make Sense* (Colorado Springs: Waterbrook Press, 2000), 9.

No Rights for the Righteous?

Some Bible teachers claim a Christian has no rights at all, and in one sense, that's true. If we call Christ "Lord," we submit ourselves to His leading wherever He may direct us. We have no right to go against the will of God. On the other hand, He has given us the right and responsibility to act appropriately in human relationships. As his beloved children, we are to be wise in our interaction with others. Jesus told us to be "wise as serpents, and harmless as doves" (Matthew 10:16). That means we should discern motives and observe actions in relationships, and respond in wisdom, but not with manipulation or revenge. When someone tries to abuse or control us, we should protect ourselves. Paul models this when he warns Timothy to beware of a man who had attacked Paul:

> *Alexander the metalworker did me a great deal of harm. The Lord will repay him for what he has done. You too should be on your guard against him, because he strongly opposed our message.*
> *(2 Timothy 4:14-15)*

173

Similarly, we need to be on guard against those who have hurt or threaten to hurt us. But being on guard doesn't mean we counterattack. Paul encouraged Timothy to keep in mind that God Himself would repay the wrong committed. It is entirely appropriate for us to protect ourselves but not to take revenge.

Since we are to submit first and foremost to the Lord and not to people, we are to obey Him at all cost and at all times. A significant question, then, is: What is the Lord's will when we find ourselves in a difficult relationship?

Many scriptures instruct us to "love one another," but many of us are confused about what it means to love an addict or an abusive person. If an alcoholic asks you for a drink, is it loving to give him a bottle? No, of course not. Providing alcohol may be submissive to the person's will, but it wouldn't be in his or her best interest, and therefore, it wouldn't be honoring to the Lord. In the same way, if a demanding, abusive, manipulative person commands you to submit, is it loving to give in? No again. The loving thing is to confront the behavior and help that person take steps toward self-control, responsibility, and kindness.

Submitting out of fear may be obeying the person's wishes, but it isn't obeying God. Ultimately, that isn't loving the person, either, because it isn't what is best for him or her. Paul wrote the Romans: "Love must be without hypocrisy" (Romans 12:9 NASB). We are hypocrites if we cower in fear as we obey an abusive person and call it "love." Genuine love is strong enough to speak the truth and do what is best for someone else, even if he or she doesn't like it. Genuine love also seeks wisdom to do the right thing, not to become a doormat or to compulsively "fix" things because we are afraid. Conversely, we are not to refuse to help simply because we are angry.

What Now?

Many dreams have died on the threshold of missed opportunity. What are the critical opportunities God has put in front of you? Is He speaking to you about the next step in your walk with Him? Is there a ministry possibility that you need to grab? Is there an idol in your heart you need to destroy?

In some cases, like strained relationships, the opportunity to respond is constantly in front of us, but for others the window closes fairly quickly. The new trapeze bar doesn't swing toward us forever. We have to grab it when it's there, or it'll be gone. Only on rare occasions do our *chronos* and God's *kairos* intersect, so we need to be ready when the convergence happens. Too many fractured relationships aren't mended simply because someone didn't have the courage to say, "I'm sorry," or "I forgive you." Many people haven't come to Christ because we've found it inconvenient to take the time to talk with them. Forgiveness has its timing. Don't miss a chance to let it liberate you.

Years ago, I was setting up a meeting room for a conference and asked a hotel worker, "Sir, do you think it's possible that we could get a pot of coffee in here for our meeting?"

> Genuine love is strong enough to speak the truth.

The man instantly smiled and told me, "Yes, sir. Everything is possible."

What a great example of the "hospitality industry" in action! If a hotel worker has that kind of attitude about his job, what expectation should we have as we follow the One whose power flung billions of stars into space and whose love was demonstrated in the ultimate revelation of grace at the cross! Does your situation look hopeless? Jesus said, "What is impossible with men is possible with God" (Luke 18:27).

He forgave you extravagantly, and He will help you forgive others extravagantly. Ask God to show you the forgiveness bar you need to grab, and take hold for all it's worth.

Think Outside the Box

1. *What are the main points of Jesus' parable of the two servants in Matthew 18? Have you ever acted like the first servant? If so, what was the result? What kind of "torture" did you experience?*

2. *As you've observed family and friends, what are some of the consequences of refusing to forgive those who have caused harm?*

3. *How does bitterness give us identity and energy? Are these "benefits" worth it? Why or why not?*

4. *Think of the reasons people refuse to forgive. Which ones stand out to you as most common or reasonable? Which ones have you used?*

5. *Describe the connections and the differences between forgiveness and trust.*

6. *As you've read this chapter, has the Lord brought to mind anyone you need to forgive? Is there anyone whose forgiveness you need to seek? When will you act on God's prompting?*

7. *Your willingness, desire, and ability to forgive others who have hurt you will only begin when God makes you aware of the amazing depths to which He went to rescue you. Have you forgotten? Have you ever been aware of His amazing forgiveness for your own sins? You'll never be able to give mercy and grace to others until you realize how much you've received. Spend some time reliving the events surrounding your testimony. Remember where you were, where you were going, and what you were when the Lord saved you.*

life's most valuable lessons

God wants to use every moment in our lives—the good and the bad—to shape our character and deepen our faith. The goal isn't to get rid of our painful past (that can't happen), but to let God use it for good. In his book, *The Healing Path*, psychologist Dan Allender describes the spiritual perception we can have about painful events in our lives:

> *If we fail to anticipate thoughtfully how we will respond to the harm of living in a fallen world, the pain may be for naught. It will either numb or destroy us rather than refine and even bless us. . . . Healing in this life is not the resolution of our past; it is the use of our past to draw us into deeper relationship with God and His purposes for our lives.*[39]

Fallen—Into God's Plan

We can't escape living in a fallen world. Like Jesus, we weep over death, disease, divorce, and many other wounds in our lives and the lives of those we love. And like Jesus, we know there's hope for healing and change. In the loving hands of Jesus, wounds that have terrified us become the source of

---

39. Dan Allender, *The Healing Path* (Colorado Springs: Water Brook Press, 1999), 5-6.

our deepest insights and the platform for our most effective ministry to others. Compassion simply can't be produced in a vacuum. God shapes it in us as He heals our hurts and as we forgive those who have offended us. If we trust God to heal us, our deepest pain is the doorway to our greatest spiritual growth and ministry.

> **Pain is a passport into the hearts of people around us.**

Pain is a passport into the hearts of people around us. When I sit next to people on a plane, I rarely tell them I'm a pastor. That label raises red flags and sets off warning sirens. I just talk to them about life, and, quite often, something painful comes up in the conversation. One person may be in the middle of a divorce, another has a deathly sick child, and another endures strained relationships or disappointments at work. Whatever the story, I often tell a little of the pain I've experienced, and we comfort one another. If my seatmate discovers I'm a pastor, he or she often says something like, "Wow, you're almost normal! If I lived near you, I'd come to your church." I take that as a compliment to the healing power of the Spirit in my life. Years ago, I thought all of my pain, dysfunction, and shame threatened to disqualify me from ministry, but now I see that these things actually validate me. They're part of God's extravagant work in me and often open doors into the lives of people I meet.

The biblical story of Joseph illustrates how this works. Jacob's eleventh son, Joseph was the most loved of the boys. His father's preferential treatment, not surprisingly, inflamed his brothers' jealousy. They sold him to Ishmaelites who traded him in Egypt, and, once there, he had to flee the seductions of his master's wife. Joseph was unjustly thrown in prison and remained there for years until God miraculously spared his life and placed him in a position of power over all of Egypt. Thanks to Joseph's administrative genius, the nation was saved from starvation. During the famine for which Joseph had prepared Pharaoh's people, Jacob sent several sons south to Egypt to buy food. There, Joseph hid his identity and tested his brothers to see if they had changed. When they passed the tests, he revealed his identity. They were amazed he was still alive, let alone that he was the prime minister of Egypt! When their father died, the brothers feared Joseph would take revenge, but Joseph assured them:

> *Don't be afraid. Am I in the place of God? You intended to harm me, but God intended it for good to accomplish what is now being done, the saving of many lives. So then, don't be afraid. I will provide for you and your children. (Genesis 50:19-21)*

179

Joseph never gave up in despair during the prolonged darkness in his life. No matter what happened, he remained strong, believing God. When the time was right, God raised him to a place of honor and power. And because he was faithful, Egypt was saved and his family rescued from famine. Despite years of betrayal, slavery, and imprisonment, Joseph was convinced God had the best of plans for him. Nothing could destroy his faith that God still rules in the affairs of men and nations, and that someday, He would make things right for Joseph, too.

Beyond Toleration

Too many people live under the same roof with a spouse and kids in relationships that are, at best, like an armed truce. They don't shoot missiles at each other, but neither are they affectionate or affirming. Celeste Holm once said,

"We live by encouragement and die without it—slowly, sadly, angrily."[40]

God's people can do better than this, and in fact, His mandate is for us to truly love—not just tolerate—each other. Jesus didn't come to earth to barely accept us. He lavished us with love, fully embracing us when we were at our worst so He could convince us of His great grace. Learning to live His way is one of the most important lessons there is. It's also something we learn time and again.

In Chapter 5, we looked at some terms that help us learn the language of extravagant devotion. Extravagance isn't simply taking leaps of faith. It also involves learning to apply extravagance to relationships—even to people who don't necessarily deserve it. To display God's love in this way, we need to keep learning the language of God's kingdom. In relationships, the language sounds like:

180

- "I'm so sorry I did that (or said that). Will you forgive me?"
- "Can I help you? I've got some time."
- "Tell me more of what you're thinking."
- "I've been talking and not listening. Help me understand your point."
- "I love you so much."
- "I'm so proud of you."
- "You're great at that. I appreciate your talent and skill."

Some people might object, "Well, I don't feel like saying those things, and I don't want to be insincere, so I won't say them." In truth, that's just an excuse to keep tolerating instead of loving. For such love to take root in our lives, we

---

40. Cited by Charles R. Swindoll, *The Grace Awakening* (Nashville: Thomas Nelson, 1990), 217.

can't wait for feelings to inspire us. We are far more likely to act ourselves into a feeling than to feel ourselves into an action. If you start with the choice to use the right language or display a loving attitude, the feelings will eventually follow.

You might never know the impact of an encouraging word spoken to another person. In the depths of my alcohol addiction in high school, I was once in the process of stealing liquor out of the back room of the grocery store where I worked when the manager called for a bag-

> # Pat demonstrated the power of a spoken blessing.

ger to come up to the front and bag groceries. I hustled to the counter and stood next to Pat, the checkout clerk, and sacked the customer's groceries as fast as I could. I'd been in the middle of stealing whiskey, and I wanted to finish hiding the bottles before anybody caught me. As I finished bagging the groceries and the customer walked away, Pat put her hand on my arm, looked into my eyes, and said, "There's something different about you, Bryan. You're going to be somebody someday."

I almost laughed out loud as I thought, *Lady, if you had any idea what I'm doing in the back room of this store right now, you'd never say anything like that to me!* But her words stuck in my heart as a message from God that maybe, just maybe, He had a bigger, better plan for my life. I've never forgotten Pat's kindness and courage to speak hope into my heart when I felt completely hopeless. I didn't understand then what I know now: Pat demonstrated the power of a spoken blessing.

After my radical encounter with God a few months later, I found myself in a dilemma for which, once again, encouraging words held the answer. I was playing high school football and loving the game, but because I was working at a local bank and already preaching regularly, my schedule was a mess. I realized that if I was going to keep my grades up so I could go to college, keep my job, and follow God's calling to preach, there was only one solution: football had to go. One morning before school, I stopped by the office of my head football coach, Don Campbell. With tears streaming down my face, I told him I had to quit. I felt like a coward and a quitter, and I was ashamed that I couldn't make life work.

> It was the first time any man in authority had ever spoken a blessing over my life.

In response, Coach Campbell told me, "Bryan, I want you to stay on the team. It's not because you're the best athlete we have. Both of us know that." (He could have left that part out.) "There are some guys on our team who are going to get scholarships to play in college, but I'd trade all 62 boys on this team for one of you. Do you know why?"

I shook my head.

"Because you have heart. You don't have the size and talent some of the others do, but these players need you in their lives as an example to aspire to, and I want you to stay on this team to inspire them. Don't quit. If you have an opportunity to preach, go and preach. If you miss practice, that's okay. If you miss, I can't start you in the next game, but I won't punish you. I need you here."

Coach Campbell paused for a few seconds, then added, "Bryan, some of these young men will play college football, but *you're* going to make something of yourself. I believe in you."

You can't imagine (then again, maybe you can) what Coach Campbell's encouragement meant to me that day and every day since. He's a man's man, six feet five inches tall, a hulk of masculinity, strong in every way. When *he* said, "I believe in you," it electrified my heart and gave me more confidence than ever. It was the first time any man in authority had ever spoken a blessing over my life.

It would be hard to over-emphasize the significance of speaking sincere, positive words into someone's life, but I'll limit myself to one more personal story. In my first few weeks at Bible college, I gave a speech in one of my classes. As I left the room, the professor, Coach Hanson (she also coached the college's girls' volleyball team) stopped me and said, "Bryan, that was a magnificent speech today. By the time you graduate, they're going to ask you to speak at commencement." She stirred a spiritual gift in me by the power of her spoken blessing, and a few years later, I spoke at my college graduation. Whenever I visit the college, I usually drop by to thank her for believing in me.

Washing Away Criticism

Many of us have internalized negative input to the point it seems natural that we, in turn, are constantly critical of others. Instead of speaking blessings, our words are like sandpaper or sledgehammers, gradually eroding a person's confidence or quickly shattering it. We drink in the twin poisons of shame and self-pity, demanding that others treat us better, or being furious when they don't. Passing bitter pills to everyone in our lives becomes a pattern.

When we experience the grace of God, however, He breaks the bonds of the mentality that cries at others, "I deserve better than that!" We realize God has provided us far more grace and love than we deserve, and our demands melt into gratitude. The same transition happens in relationships. Instead of complaining that people aren't what

183

we want them to be and that they don't treat us the way we want to be treated, we can look beyond whatever barriers seem to present themselves and love others anyway.

To truly love people, we often have to clear away the garbage in our lives. One time, I prepared what I thought would be a powerful message on love from 1 Corinthians 13, but Haley and I had been fighting. I realized, though, that I couldn't preach on love when anger at my wife filled my heart.

> Honesty is the path to restored and strengthened affection.

I prayed, "Lord, what can I do?"

I heard the Lord whisper, "Wash her feet."

I thought through the logistics of getting a basin and a towel to wash her feet before we left for church, but the Spirit said, "No, Bryan. In front of everybody."

That night, before I started my sermon, I told the congregation, "Tonight, I'm preaching about love, but I've offended my wife. I've been terribly selfish, and in front of all of you, I want to ask her to forgive me. I can't preach this message until I get this right." I turned to Haley and said, "Honey, I know you don't like to be in front of people, but this is from my heart. Will you come up and let me wash your feet as an act of humility and forgiveness?"

She came to the platform, and I pulled out a basin and a towel. I washed her feet as both of us wept. We hugged, and she forgave me. That night, I preached about love with a clean heart and a clear conscience. It couldn't have happened if Haley and I had continued to merely tolerate each other and let smoldering anger burn the love out of our relationship. Our dissension had to end, and it had to end immediately.

I know plenty of husbands, wives, and parents of teenagers who are angry because the people they love resist their attempts to tell them how they should live. Every word comes across as a demand that drives a wedge of resentment deeper between them. Yet if they'd stop talking and start listening, they could rebuild trust. If they would ask questions instead of demanding compliance, they would connect with each other. If they would look for traits to affirm instead of focusing on faults, they'd build up their loved one's confidence instead of tearing it down.

When we're willing to admit we've sinned or "blown it" in some way, we may fear that a forthright admission will ruin our credibility, but quite to the contrary, it actually raises our credibility. I've seen it dozens of times—for myself and others. The people I love value and love me more when I admit I've hurt them and ask for forgiveness, but as long as I imagine they "deserved it" or that what I did really didn't hurt them, we remain distant. Honesty is the path to restored and strengthened affection.

The God Model

Remember that God exemplifies the absolute lover. He didn't just dab His love on us. He poured it out in overflowing extravagance. When we experience His kindness at the deepest levels of our lives, we have the resources and the motivation to show His love and forgiveness to the people who have hurt us and disappointed us. Bitterness over past hurts poisons the heart and ruins relationships, and merely tolerating people is a form of slow death for us all. Extravagant devotion to God unleashes the beauty of His forgiveness in our hearts. Through us, it pours into the lives of those around us. And it transforms everything it touches.

Pastor Kerry Shook wrote a book called *One Month to Live: Thirty Days to a No-Regrets Life*. He suggests that we should live as if we have only one month left, resolving every problem, showing every kind of affection, restoring every relationship, and taking every risk to honor the Lord—so we never miss an opportunity to be the person God wants us to be. We taught these principles at our church and saw amazing things happen. People who had held grudges for decades went to each other to confess their sins and ask forgiveness. They flew across the country to reconcile with a family member who had been estranged. Many simply made it a point to say "I love you" more often. Families experienced more joy, love, and laughs than they had in years. But you don't have to wait for a sermon series to see the wonders of grace blossom. They can become a new normal for anyone who longs to live an extravagant life in Christ.

You can't make people love and forgive you. You can't force reconciliation. All you can do is keep a clean heart, forgive those who have hurt you, and offer a path of restoration to those who have become distant. You aren't responsible for *their* attitude and actions, just your own. As Paul said, "If it is possible, as far as it depends on you, live at peace with everyone" (Romans 12:18).

There's no sense in denying the pain we've suffered or the wounds we've caused. We need to bring them out into the open and let the light of God's love shine on them. I was abandoned and abused, and I became an alcoholic and a thief. I was a prodigal who knew what was right but trampled the blood of Jesus under my feet. Still, God broke in to rescue me. If it weren't for His grace and power, I'd be in prison today or maybe in a grave. Not only did Jesus rescue me from hell—and the living hell of a meaningless life—He also gave me the unspeakable privilege of representing Him to other sinners who just as desperately need the touch of His love. He's also granted me the lavish gift of a beautiful family.

186

The pain I've experienced now helps me identify with the people who walk in the doors of our church each week. I've cried myself to sleep on countless nights. I've even contemplated murder. I know what it feels like to hate, and I know what it means to cower in fear. There are still scars, but the open wounds are past because of the love, power, and forgiveness of God.

One of my favorite hymns is "The Love of God" by Frederick M. Lehman. The song describes the love that enables us to forgive even those who have hurt us. Many years after he wrote this hymn, Lehman reflected on its origin. He reported that the third stanza was found written on the wall of a patient's room in an insane asylum. Lehman had heard a traveling evangelist quote the stanza at the close of a sermon on God's love, and he was so moved that he later wrote the first two stanzas and the chorus. Read the hymn, and make it your prayer of praise, wonder, and worship.[41]

The love of God is greater far
Than tongue or pen can ever tell;
It goes beyond the highest star,
And reaches to the lowest hell;
The guilty pair, bowed down with care,
God gave His Son to win;
His erring child He reconciled,
And pardoned from his sin.

Refrain
Oh, love of God, how rich and pure!
How measureless and strong!
It shall forevermore endure—
The saints' and angels' song.

---

41. Frederick M. Lehman, pamphlet: *History of the Song*, "The Love of God", 1948.

When hoary time shall pass away,
And earthly thrones and kingdoms fall,
When men who here refuse to pray,
On rocks and hills and mountains call,
God's love so sure, shall still endure,
All measureless and strong;
Redeeming grace to Adam's race—
The saints' and angels' song.

Could we with ink the ocean fill,
And were the skies of parchment made,
Were every stalk on earth a quill,
And every man a scribe by trade;
To write the love of God above
Would drain the ocean dry;
Nor could the scroll contain the whole,
*   Though stretched from sky to sky.*[42]

Think Outside the Box

1. *How have you seen a person's pain become a passport into the lives of others to show them the compassion and love of God? Has your pain become a passport for you? How so?*
2. *What are some differences between tolerating someone and truly loving him or her?*
3. *Do you make it a point to speak positive words into the lives of others? Can you think of someone who needs that from you right now?*
4. *Is there someone in your life whose feet you need to wash—either literally or figuratively?*

---

42. Lehman, "The Love of God," 1917.

5.   *What would it mean for you to live and love like you only have thirty days left to live? How would you live differently than you do now?*

chapter 17

the call to extravagance

During my times of particular extravagance—the year I went without a salary, the time Haley and I gave up our house, and my stint of working two jobs—I saw God work just as extraordinarily in other people's lives. A few gave their houses, too. One man donated his antique car collection. People presented four-wheelers and shotguns, silverware from a family plantation of generations ago, and an autographed Beatles album. One rising music star even gave the church his tour bus.

During my no-salary year, the generosity of our people enabled the church to pay off an exorbitant debt in just eleven months. All this happened in a depressed economy and in a community with a median household income just above $27,000 per year, a poverty rate of more than 25 percent, and only 33 percent functional literacy.[43] It was miraculous!

Genuine extravagance always amazes people, but amid all the energy it creates, it's critical to remember *why* we're extravagant. We display extravagant devotion to God because He is *precious* to us—more precious than whatever we devote to His purposes—and the spillover effects are wonderful. Our display of affection is *pleasant* to others, *perplexing* to some, and *pleasing* to God.

---

43. U.S. Census Bureau, Arkansas, http://quickfacts.census.gov/qfd/states/05/0555310.html.

Mary's Extravagance

The gospel writers give us a beautiful picture of one woman's extravagant response to Jesus at a dinner party with two sisters, Mary and Martha, and their brother Lazarus. Matthew and Mark tell us that the meal took place in Bethany at the home of Simon the Leper, or more likely, "the former leper," because I'm fairly certain Jesus would have healed him. (Plus, no one would eat dinner in the home of a contagious leper.) John explains that not long before the dinner, the people gathered had been traumatized by a death in the family, but Jesus had performed a miracle. Lazarus had become gravely ill and died. A few days after he was buried, Jesus arrived, asked those present to roll the stone away from Lazarus' tomb, and Mary's and Martha's beloved brother walked out into the sunlight. Now, they were at Simon's home for a dinner to celebrate and to honor Jesus. John paints the scene:

> Our extravagance is a response to God's first and bigger extravagant display of love.

192

> *Martha served, while Lazarus was among those reclining at the table with him. Then Mary took about a pint of pure nard, an expensive perfume; she poured it on Jesus' feet and wiped his feet with her hair. And the house was filled with the fragrance of the perfume. (John 12:2-3)*

The dinner event—and Mary's extreme act that made it so memorable—exemplifies all the traits of extravagant devotion.

Precious to Us

We learn later in the account that the jar of perfume was incredibly valuable, worth a year's salary for an average worker. It may well have been the most precious thing Mary owned. But notice that she didn't just dab on a little and save most of it for other times. She emptied the whole jar on Jesus' feet, uncovered her hair, and wiped his feet with her locks. Saving up to buy that perfume may have taken years, but Mary poured it out in a few seconds. What caused her to be so extravagant in her affection? Likely, she was overwhelmed with gratitude because Jesus had given her brother back to her.

Mary's not alone. I've noticed that every act of extravagant devotion recounted in the Bible (and there are many) is prompted by a heart overflowing with gratitude for the grace, mercy, and provision of God. Our extravagance is a response to God's first and bigger extravagant display of love. When Jesus is precious to us, we can't help but pour out our gratitude in unmeasured ways. That response is a natural reaction.

The reason worship in our churches is often so anemic, our giving stingy, and our service so sporadic is that we don't fully grasp the depth and breadth of God's immeasurable grace. Yet we shouldn't have to see someone physically raised from the dead to appreciate God's extravagant love. We just need to look in the mirror and be honest about what we find. None of us came to God with anything that would impress Him. He owed us nothing at all, but He gave us a free gift of forgiveness and life.

We may be masters at fooling other people, but God knows our hearts. And when we're honest with ourselves, we recognize the depths of our selfishness and depravity. A heart of gratitude develops when we realize we are more wicked than we ever imagined, but God's grace has given us a place at His table we never deserved. He shouldn't have to do anything else for us to elicit a response of extravagant praise and gratitude. He doesn't have to give us a great job, heal a family member, bring home a prodigal child, or mend a broken relationship to prove that He loves us. He's already raised us from the pit of hell, and that's enough. If we keep in mind what we really deserve but what God has done to save us, we'll be like Mary every day. The flood of thanksgiving and praise can't be stopped!

Paul's letter to the Ephesians provides one of Scripture's most beautiful descriptions of the grace of God. He points out that we were dead, helpless and hopeless apart from Christ, and then he writes:

> *But because of his great love for us, God, who is rich in mercy, made us alive with Christ even when we were dead in transgressions—it is by grace you have been saved. And God raised us up with Christ and seated us with him in the heavenly realms in Christ Jesus, in order that in the coming ages he might show the incomparable riches of his grace, expressed in his kindness to us in Christ Jesus. (Ephesians 2:4-7)*

194

We offer nothing; we receive everything. Christ's love is great, His mercy rich, and His kindness amazing. Jesus is precious beyond words, and Mary's heart wouldn't let her settle for a mediocre response to the love He offered her.

What about you? When was the last time you went beyond mediocrity in prayer, worship, giving, fasting, forgiving, loving, and serving? Are you content to do the least you can for God, or does your heart long to spend and be spent in an extravagant display of gratitude, no matter what anyone thinks of you? Mary surrendered all to Jesus because He was more precious to her than anything else in the world.

Pleasant to Others

Mary's gift to Jesus was delightful to others. The aroma of perfume filled the house and wafted down the street into the homes of neighbors. Her affection for Jesus warmed the hearts of everyone (well, almost everyone) there. When we give ourselves unreservedly to God, people detect the aroma of life in us. Many long for it, a few despise it, but no one can deny it.

Far too often, our neighbors and co-workers don't see anything different in us. They're confused when they discover that we go to church because they don't notice Jesus in us. Yet when the love of Christ possesses

> His life in us spills into the lives of those around us.

and overwhelms us, the way we talk, think, and act changes. His life in us spills into the lives of those around us. For Mary, who had been possessed by an evil spirit, it became a joyous relief to be possessed by the Spirit of God.

I can imagine the testimonies of at least two of the men around the dining table that day. Guys love to one-up each other with stories of bigger fish, better athletic plays, and more profitable clients, so as the disciples and friends celebrated over dinner Jesus' power to change lives, I can almost hear Simon telling everyone, "I was a leper. You should have seen my skin. Okay, okay, I won't talk about it at dinner, but you gotta know, Jesus *made me whole.*" In reply, Lazarus would have announced, "Yeah, well, have you ever been dead before? Jesus *brought me out of a hole in the ground!*" Jesus and the rest of the people probably got a kick out of this banter because the whole scene was a celebration of Jesus' goodness.

Perplexing to Some

Maybe when Mary got up from her place at the table and came around to anoint Jesus, it felt a bit awkward to the rest of people, but I'd guess the expression of joy on Jesus' face put most of the party at ease so they could enjoy the moment. But not everybody. Judas was a glass-half-empty guy if there ever was one. He could find something wrong with a bowl of ice cream on a summer evening. The "one who would betray Him" complained (probably in a stage whisper so that everyone could hear), "Why wasn't this perfume sold and the money given to the poor? It was worth a year's wages" (John 12:5). The truth is, Judas didn't give a rip about poor people. He just wanted the funds put in the group's moneybag so he could steal it.

> The most important feature of extravagant devotion is that it delights the heart of God.

196

In conversations with various people over the years, Jesus let a lot of foolish things pass without commenting or correcting them, but not this time. In a week, He would be nailed to a cross. He knew Mary's perfume would be the only formal anointing for His burial. Others would run, but Mary would stay. He turned to Judas and chided:

> *Leave her alone. Why are you bothering her?*
> *She has done a beautiful thing to me. The poor*
> *you will always have with you, and you can*
> *help them any time you want. But you will not*
> *always have me. She did what she could. She*
> *poured perfume on my body beforehand to pre-*
> *pare for my burial. I tell you the truth, wherever*
> *the gospel is preached throughout the world,*

*what she has done will also be told, in memory
of her.* (Mark 14:6-9)

Mary's extravagance captured the heart of God.

Not everyone appreciates extravagant devotion. Mary did; Judas didn't. To be sure, when we pour out our hearts, our treasure, and our talents in an abundant show of how much we adore God, a few people will think we're crazy. The human heart—others' or ours—resists extravagance and wants to tone down lavish displays of any kind. Folks who are uncomfortable with lavish devotion will accuse us of being "excessive," "unrealistic," or "extreme." But that's okay. Virtually every extravagant display of devotion toward God has taken flack from a few. It's up to our faith in God's appreciation to remember that unrestrained expressions please our Lord and unleash His blessings like nothing else can. Jesus always notices our affection for Him, and He will honor us.

In churches and homes across the globe, we still read the story of Mary's outpouring of love and gratitude. As Scripture promised, her act has gone down in history as a permanent testimony of her heartfelt, effusive—and reasonable—devotion.

Pleasing to Christ

The most important feature of extravagant devotion is that it delights the heart of God. Jesus' defense of Mary against Judas' attack gives us a glimpse of Jesus' joy over Mary's outpouring of love. The Lord never ignores our hidden prayers, heartfelt concern for others, or the glad service we offer when no one is looking. The psalmist tells us, God "inhabits the praises" of His people (Psalm 22:3). He longs to live in the splendid atmosphere of our surrender, obedience, courage, and love for Him.

Author Phillip Keller presents a fresh perspective about what's "written between the lines" in the gospel accounts. He suggests that, in the momentous week following the dinner at Simon's house, when Jesus argued with religious leaders in the temple, healed sick people, and prepared His men to take over after He had gone back to the Father, the aroma of Mary's perfume stayed with Him. The memory of her devotion followed Him—in the courtyard of the temple, in the room where He celebrated Passover with His men, to the Garden of Gethsemane, into Herod's hall, in the court of the Sanhedrin, onto Pilate's patio, on the dusty streets as He carried the cross, and as He hung dying. The sweet smell had penetrated His clothes, His skin, and His hair, and every day, it reminded Him that at least one faithful person loved Him enough to prepare Him for burial. Others may have wanted things *from* Him, but Mary wanted nothing more than to give something *to* Him.[44]

Although the gospel writers don't tell us about the lingering aroma of Mary's perfume in those last hours of Jesus' earthly life, maybe He smelled it a bit more when they pressed the crown of thorns on His head, when the sweat of His brow unleashed a few droplets of it as He staggered under the cross, and the wind brought it to His nose as He was suspended between heaven and earth. It's conceivable that Mary's extravagant gift of costly perfume gave Jesus strength to face His suffering and death. Her extravagance sustained *Him*.

Too Busy for Devotion

We find Mary at center stage three different times in the gospels. Each time, she humbled herself at the feet of Jesus. Once, when Jesus and His band visited Bethany, Martha cooked dinner while Mary sat listening to Jesus. Although

---

44. W. Phillip Keller, *Rabboni: Which Is to Say, Master* (Kregel Publications, 1997), 200.

her sister wanted Mary to break away and help with dinner preparations, Mary knew what was more important. When Lazarus was sick, Mary sent for Jesus to come and heal her brother. Upon Jesus' delayed arrival, Mary ran to ask why He hadn't come sooner. Her heart was broken, but she affirmed her faith even through her tears. And here at Simon's dinner, she was again at the feet of Jesus, this time pouring out her love from a jar of expensive perfume. Every time we see her, she's close to Jesus, at his feet listening, learning, weeping, and anointing. She *lived* at the feet of Jesus—in times of sorrow, instruction, and joy. Nothing kept her from Him.

> Observing Mary's intense devotion has touched me deeply.

Observing Mary's intense devotion has touched me deeply. At the end of my life, I don't want people to say that I was primarily a good father, a fine husband, a reliable friend, or a dynamic pastor. I want them to notice one key characteristic about me. I want them to say, "Bryan lived at the feet of Jesus and really knew the Lord. He was a man of extravagant devotion."

Jesus had told His disciples many times that He would be killed in Jerusalem. He explained that His death is the main reason He came to earth. But they didn't understand. Even on the last night before His betrayal, Jesus told them several times that He was about to be arrested, tried, tortured, and executed, but they still didn't get it. Yet even though Mary had spent far less time with Jesus than His disciples, she had a level of spiritual insight that enabled her to understand His purpose. As she poured perfume on His feet, Jesus said to the people watching, "It was intended that she should save this perfume for the day of my burial"

(Mark 14:8). That day had come, and she was ready. I believe God gives unusual spiritual insight to those who display extravagant devotion to Him—like Mary.

In our society, one of the biggest hindrances to a life of extravagant devotion is that we're absurdly busy. We think it's a virtue to cram every second with work, hobbies, television, music, and talk. I know, I know: these things aren't necessarily bad. In fact, most of them are essential to a degree. But if they consume all of our time, they prevent us from thinking, pondering, and praying so that the truth of God's word and the love of His heart can penetrate our crust. Author Richard Foster argues that this obstacle is, in fact, part of the cosmic spiritual battle we fight: "Our Adversary majors in three things: noise, hurry and crowds. If he can keep us engaged in 'muchness' and 'manyness,' he will rest satisfied."[45] Renowned psychotherapist Carl Jung similarly observed, "Hurry is not of the devil, hurry is the devil."[46]

> One of the biggest hindrances to a life of extravagant devotion is that we're absurdly busy.

200

Slowing down so that we have the mental space to reflect is not an option for those who want to know Christ. It's an absolute necessity. Over the centuries, believers have developed habits to help them tap into God's truth and love. These habits are often called "spiritual disciplines" and methods to prepare our hearts to listen more acutely to God's voice. The most common ones used by evangelical believers are prayer, Bible study and memorization, service

---

45. Richard Foster, *Celebration of Discipline* (San Francisco: HarperCollins, 1988), 15.
46. Cited by Gary W. Moon, *Apprenticeship with Jesus: Learning to Live Like the Master* (Grand Rapids: Baker Books, 2009), 208.

to others, meditating on Scripture, fasting, silence, and solitude. In his insightful book, *The Life You've Always Wanted*,
John Ortberg reminds us of the purpose of these habits:

> *Spiritual disciplines are not about trying to be
> good enough to merit God's forgiveness and
> goodwill. They are not ways to get extra credit,
> or to demonstrate to God how deeply we are
> committed to him.... But spiritual disciplines
> are simply a means of appropriating or growing
> toward the life that God graciously offers. This
> is why they are sometimes called "a means of
> grace."*[47]

The motivation to develop these habits is important. We
begin with appropriate disappointment over our current
spiritual condition and a longing for more. Ortberg isolates
the source of this discontent with our spirituality:

> *Where does this disappointment come from? A
> common answer in our day is that it is a lack of
> self-esteem, a failure to accept oneself. . . . The
> older and wiser answer is that the feeling of
> disappointment is not the problem, but a reflec-
> tion of a deeper problem—my failure to be the
> person God had in mind when he created me. It
> is the "pearly ache" in my heart to be at home
> with the Father.*[48]

Bear in mind that, if a greater measure of spiritual discipline is new to you, you shouldn't expect perfection right
away. When any of us learn how to use something new—a

201

47. John Ortberg, *The Life You've Always Wanted* (Grand Rapids: Zondervan, 2002), 46-47.
48. Ibid. 13.

software program, a complicated recipe, or a power tool—the learning curve can be steep. The process of becoming competent follows the same path I explained earlier—from unconsciously unskilled to unconsciously skilled.

Some believers mistakenly think that the first time they do real Bible study, carve out an hour to pray, fast for a day or two, or block off a Saturday to serve at a homeless shelter, they'll feel the tingle of the Holy Spirit and walk away with insights no one but Jesus and Paul ever had before! But that seldom happens. A realistic understanding of the development required in spiritual discipline helps overcome initial discomfort, confusion, and apparent lack of tangible results. The richest veins of gold are often found deepest in the earth. The diligent miners—only the ones with fierce determination—eventually uncover wealth beyond imagination. Rewards come to those who stay committed to spiritual discipline and growth.

Hearing the Voice of God

For me, it's easy to dive into the more active spiritual disciplines of Bible study, prayer, fellowship, and service. Yet the ones that have meant the most to my spiritual vitality—the ones that are the hardest for a compulsively energetic person like me—are those that steal me away from busyness, slow me down, and create space for me to listen to the voice of God. The disciplines of silence, solitude, and fasting have revolutionized my relationship with God.

When television stations around the country made the switch from analog to digital signals, one station posted this helpful statement: "If you're having trouble with your new signal, contact the station for assistance." A lot of good that would do! Like these poor television owners, if we don't have the right equipment, we can't even hear the warnings. To hear the voice of God, I believe we need the "equipment" of silence and solitude.

Jesus modeled the importance of getting away from the rat race to be refreshed and restored so He could go back into the fray at full strength. The disciples often found Him alone on a hillside or a mountaintop in prayer to the Father, and He sometimes took His men on retreats to rest and get a fresh perspective on their calling.

The question is: Do you really believe God still speaks to us today, or was that all in the days of Moses, the prophets, and Jesus? The answer is emphatically: He does. Jesus is called "the Word," and the Bible "the word of God." These terms reveal that it is God's nature to communicate with His creation, and especially to those who have entered into a relationship with Him.

The richest veins of gold are often found deepest in the earth.

Jesus explained this powerful and intimate relationship in terms the people of His day understood clearly. In their agrarian society, raising sheep was a way of life for thousands of people, so they knew some traits of the animals Jesus so often used in analogy to human beings. Several flocks, for instance, might mingle together in a pen, but the voice of each shepherd was enough to separate the flocks. When a given herder called, his sheep would leave the others to go with him. Jesus explained:

> *The man who enters by the gate is the shepherd of his sheep. The watchman opens the gate for him, and the sheep listen to his voice. He calls his own sheep by name and leads them out. When he has brought out all his own, he goes*

on ahead of them, and his sheep follow him because they know his voice. (John 10:2-4)

Jesus is always speaking, but we're not always listening.

Another reason the quieter spiritual disciplines are so important is that God seldom yells to get our attention. He whispers. If we're too distracted by the noise of life, we simply can't hear God's voice. We have to get away, clear our minds and hearts, and block out distractions. Success in business or ministry doesn't guarantee that we'll become good listeners. In fact, success can be our biggest hindrance. Elijah, who had been used by God to present some of the greatest miracles recorded in the Bible, is an example of how success can hinder us. During Elijah's ministry, God had sent ravens to provide food for him, He caused a widow's jug of oil to never run dry, and in a fantastic display of power, God sent down fire to consume a water-drenched offering. Even the rocks of the altar were consumed at Elijah's hand to prove that Yahweh was greater than the god Baal! After these incredible displays of God's miraculous power, however, the prophet became deeply depressed and afraid. As he hid in the mountains, God came to him and asked simply, "What are you doing here, Elijah?"

The great prophet responded with a whine, "I've been very zealous for the Lord God Almighty, but the Israelites have rejected your covenant, broken down your altars, and put your prophets to death with the sword. I am the only one left, and now they are trying to kill me, too." At that, God told Elijah to stand on the mountain and watch for His presence to pass by:

> **Jesus is always speaking, but we're not always listening.**

Then a great and powerful wind tore the moun-
tains apart and shattered the rocks before the
Lord, but the Lord was not in the wind. After
the wind there was an earthquake, but the Lord
was not in the earthquake. After the earthquake
came a fire, but the Lord was not in the fire. And
after the fire came a gentle whisper. When Elijah
heard it, he pulled his cloak over his face and
went out and stood at the mouth of the cave. (1
Kings 19:11-13)

God still whispers. We need to recognize the clutter of noise
and activity in our lives. When we engage in silence and
solitude, we discover the multitude of inner distractions
we've allowed to consume us: negative emotions, secret desires, painful memories, anxieties, fear of losing someone's
approval, the compulsion to accomplish things, and many
others. We can't control these thoughts by sheer strength
of will. They have to be replaced by God's grace and truth.
Getting quiet and alone enables us to see the world more
clearly. As the saying goes, "Muddy water only becomes
clear if you let it be still for a while." And if we carve out
time for silence and solitude, we learn to hear the voice of
God. As we draw close to Him, He convinces us that we are
more valuable to Him than all the wealth of the world, and
He longs to reveal more of Himself to us.

As I described most notably in Chapter 6, God has used
times of fasting in the past few years to heighten my spiritual awareness and enable me to experience extended times
of silence and solitude. There's something about starving
the flesh that feeds the spirit. When hunger pangs gnaw at
me, I pray, "Lord, let my spirit long for you as much as my
body yearns for food!" This is a common biblical theme. In
the middle of intense suffering and confusion, Job said, "I
desire your word, Lord, more than my daily bread." *That's*

the spirit of fasting. When we go without food for an extended time, our senses become more alive. We realize our desperate need for God, and we sense His presence more intimately.

As we clear away distractions, we find clarity about direction and intensify our requests of God. We experience brokenness and sorrow over our depraved hearts, and we realize more than ever that we are gloriously loved, forgiven, and accepted through the blood of Christ. Going without food for a while heightens our dependence on God and opens communication channels with Him. It's a practice worth developing for all of us.

God will speak to us, but only if we are wise enough to create undistracted, quiet time and space that will allow us to hear His voice. Quiet is essential, but it's just a prerequisite. In order that we will do what we hear God direct, Scripture points out that we must have a heart to obey. God delights in revealing Himself, but only to those who have made a commitment to actually do what He tells them to do. On the night Jesus was betrayed, He explained this principle to His men:

> *Whoever has my commands and obeys them, he*
> *is the one who loves me. He who loves me will*
> *be loved by my Father, and I too will love him*
> *and show myself to him.* (John 14:21)

"All this silence and solitude sounds great," you may think. "But what if I'm already busy doing things for God?"

It's inconceivable that God would give us so much to do that we don't have time to spend time pursuing Him. Remember Mary at Jesus' feet. Martha was the one "serving Him," but Jesus praised Mary's priority on simply being with Him. If distractions and busyness keep you from time with God, you can be fairly sure that you're doing things—

at least some things—He hasn't called you to do. The proof of a genuine desire to know God is the diligent pursuit of Him, and that pursuit always involves clearing away distractions.

Some people also wonder how they can know when they've heard the voice of God, and I can offer a few guidelines. God's message to us is always full of grace and truth, always in alignment with His Word, and is so persistent that it won't let us alone until we choose to obey. What He says is not always comfortable, but it always leads us to a deeper experience of His love, forgiveness, power, and presence.

> If we carve out time for silence and solitude, we learn to hear the voice of God.

207

I've been asked many times, "Bryan, what do you consider your most effective spiritual gift?" They expect me to say "preaching and teaching," but that's not what I tell them. As important as my ministry is to me, if I had to make a choice between losing my hearing or my ability to speak, I'd give up my voice in a heartbeat. God's greatest gift to me is the capacity to hear His voice so I can be a responsive, obedient, loving son.

A House Provided

Wherever we are in seeking God, our extravagance of devotion never outstrips His extravagance of appreciation. And a wondrous added benefit of God's response is the way He sometimes builds the interdependence of believers in Christian community.

When Haley and I gave away our house and money, we first thought of it as our individual act of devotion. The story that unfolded over the several years that followed, though, demonstrates the breadth of God's miraculous response to our faithfulness.

Haley and I downsized the family into a home with less than half the room of the dream house we'd already gotten used to, but our rented space became home. The peace of knowing we'd obeyed our loving Father made contentment with the lower standard of living easier than we expected. We focused only on the riches of ministry and family life until one day in the third year after our big giveaway, the "rest of the story" of our extravagance for God began to play out before our eyes.

> "When I was building this house, I wondered if I was building it for you."

My travels around town often took me through one particular, recently developed, upscale neighborhood. I was driving through "as usual" one day when something about a house I'd seen many times suddenly struck me as unusual. I noticed that a magnificent home Haley and I had seen in its early stages of construction two years before was still for sale. Every other house built as the neighborhood developed had been sold. Yet this showpiece remained on the market.

Haley and I had loved the house since the first time we saw the framework coming together, so on a lark, I called the phone number on the sign to see what I could find out about the situation. Right away, the voice on the line sounded familiar, and I quickly discovered that it belonged to a family connected with my church. The man told me his son, a high-end residential contractor, had built the house as one of his speculative projects when he was first developing the neighborhood, but it had never sold. He suggested that I talk with him directly.

I called the son right away, but he had little to say except to ask that I meet him at the house as soon as possible. The next day we stood in the spectacular kitchen of a dream house beyond dream houses, and Greg told me the extraordinary story that had brought us together that day.

Nearly three years earlier, Greg had visited the Sunday morning Haley and I deeded our house to the church. Although his parents attended regularly, Greg and his wife came only occasionally. Despite his interest in spiritual things, in fact, he had spent little time in church at all. Yet that morning, God touched an extravagant chord in Greg's heart that changed his life—and mine.

At the time, Greg worked for a builder who had excited in him a vision to one day begin his own construction business. He dreamed of building fine homes and had painstakingly saved $10,000 to launch his venture. That morning in our church, however, Greg felt God tugging at his heart to lay his future plans in his heavenly Father's hands. The aspiring builder emptied the savings account earmarked for his construction business and turned all $10,000 over to the church. It was a thoroughly unreasonable show of devotion, yet after that extravagant moment in Greg's life, doors of opportunity flew open for the entrepreneurial young man. Within two years, he became one of the most sought-after builders of luxury homes in the Dallas-Ft. Worth metroplex. His dream of creating multi-million dollar residences exploded into reality.

Greg gestured at the dream kitchen in which we were standing. "When I was building this house," he paused, suppressing tears, "I wondered if I was building it for you."

I just stared at the man who had rarely come back to our church since that momentous Sunday nearly three years earlier. *What a ludicrous idea*, I thought. *If Haley and I had sold our dream house and reinvested every dime, we*

209

couldn't afford a house half this nice, let alone in the situation we're in now.

"Pastor, I know you need a place to live," Greg continued, "and I've been carrying this house on my books for over two years now. The bank is more than anxious for me to pay off the construction loan. I think this is a God moment, and if you and Haley will move in here, we'll work something out."

I listened, sensing there was more Greg wanted to say.

"This is reminding me that I've become caught up in my success, and I've forgotten where it came from. Maybe this house has been sitting empty for two and a half years waiting for you to show up here."

I'm glad I showed up because what we worked out was a way for Haley and me to buy that house for pennies on the dollar. No matter how extravagant we had tried to be in giving away our dream home—and Greg in handing over his seed money—God outdid us all in the extravagance of His response. Extravagant devotion touches God's heart, and He touches us—and others—back.

Think Outside the Box

1. *Like Mary emptying the alabaster jar of perfume on Jesus' feet, what's the most extravagant display of devotion you've ever witnessed in someone else? In your own life?*
2. *How is an extravagant outpouring of love for Christ precious to us, pleasant to others, perplexing to some, and pleasing to God?*
3. *Do busyness and hurry rob you of the ability to reflect deeply and listen to God? If so, explain the results.*
4. *Which spiritual disciplines are a regular part of your life? What effect do they have on your heart, relationships, choices, and experience of God?*

5. *What are some benefits of solitude, silence, and fasting? How can you begin (or go to a deeper level) in experiencing these?*

6. *Do you expect to hear the voice of God in a consistent, powerful way? Why or why not?*

7. *How can you tell if you're open to the Spirit and willing to take bold steps of faith? Do you sense His whisper now?*

8. *How did you react to the story of God providing a house?*

chapter 18

no matter what

Spiritual life is dynamic, not static. God's work in our lives changes, depending on what we need for growth at any given point on our journey with Him. In working out His plans for us, God uses difficulties and darkness to get our attention and teach us important lessons. As we grow in our relationship with Him, we depend less and less on dramatic evidences of His presence. On this point, Dallas Willard and Jan Johnson, in *Hearing God Through the Year*, observe:

> *As Bible history proceeds, we notice that in the process of divine communication, the greater the maturity of the listener, the greater the clarity of the message and the lesser the role played by dreams, visions, and other strange phenomena and altered states.*"[49]

Sometimes, God doesn't even seem to be present at all. That's when we have to trust in the unseen instead of the seen and rely on the eternal nature of God we've come to know through Scripture rather than demanding His tangible presence. When we trust God in the dark, I believe God smiles even more.

---

49. Dallas Willard and Jan Johnson, *Hearing God Through the Year* (Downers Grove, IL: InterVarsity Press, 2004), 140.

Our relationship with God isn't a business deal. Some of us misunderstand the promises of prosperity and think that if we make enough deposits (of praise, giving, and other spiritual practices), God is obligated to protect us from all harm and give us everything we want. Sooner or later, this misguided expectation results in frustration and despair.

> We accept God's answer, even if it doesn't meet our expectation.

My son provided an amusing lesson for me about how wrong our expectations of God can be. Not quite three years old, Gavyn was already a negotiator. Riding in the car beside me one evening, he decided he wanted a Coke to drink. In my parental wisdom, I refused his request, recognizing that a sugary, caffeine-laden drink would not serve him well so close to bedtime. Gavyn, though, was not deterred and began to cry.

214

Realizing quickly that he was not making any headway in getting his wish, he paused to outline the transaction that was in process. "Okay, Dad," he explained, "here's the deal: You're the dad. I'm the kid. I'm supposed to ask for things, and you're supposed to say 'no.' Then I cry, and you say 'yes'."

It didn't work that way for Gavyn with me, and it doesn't work that way for us with God. We accept God's answer, even if it doesn't meet our expectation. Because God (the Father) knows best.

Faith Challenge

I'm always inspired when I think about the predicament of three young Jewish men who faced death in a fiery furnace because they refused to bow down before a statue of their pagan king. They answered the king's demand:

> *O Nebuchadnezzar, we do not need to defend ourselves before you in this matter. If we are thrown into the blazing furnace, the God we serve is able to save us from it, and he will rescue us from your hand, O king. But even if he does not, we want you to know, O king, that we will not serve your gods or worship the image of gold you have set up. (Daniel 3:16-18)*

These guys had no guarantee of deliverance from a horrible death, just a steadfast faith to trust God no matter what the outcome.

Stories like Nebuchadnezzar's furnace challenge me, and I enjoy challenges. Foregoing a year's salary and giving away our house made me feel more spiritually alive! But God's plan for my life isn't a continual series of knee-knocking adventures. I'm a compulsive, driven go-getter, but sometimes God tells me to do the hardest possible thing: wait for Him. I may feel ready to head into the next great challenge, but God has shown me that I shouldn't go anywhere until the pillar of fire and the cloud move. While waiting, I need to be faithful and content knowing He's called me to stay on "pause." An adrenaline rush of a new thrill every day may appeal, but God's word to me is: "Trust Me." And that's enough. I don't want to lag behind when God is leading, but neither do I want to run ahead of God when He isn't. I want to run, walk, or crawl close to His side, wherever and whenever He leads.

Like Abraham, we sometimes experience long periods of time between the promise and the miracle. We have to be patient to wait for Isaac instead of birthing an Ishmael. During times of waiting, we can be plagued with doubts about God, questions about His leading, and self-doubt about our ability to hear Him. God's delays, however, are never the denial of His promises. In times of darkness and waiting, we have to depend on what we learned about God in the light. Then we'll be ready to take the next right step.

Years ago, a young man gave me a copy of his mother's diary. She was dying of cancer, but in every journal entry, she wrote about faith on her trek to meet God. She often repeated the statement, "I can't wait until midnight." As she got weaker, she wrote only one word: "Midnight." I asked her son what this word meant to his mother, wondering if, perhaps, she received morphine every night at that time to relieve her suffering.

He laughed and told me, "No, pastor. She was convinced that God's compassions never fail. 'They are new every morning. Great is His faithfulness.' If she could just make it until midnight, His mercy in her life would be renewed again. She looked forward to that moment every day."

This dear woman had learned to trust God in the dark, confident He would provide all she needed each day.

Courage and Joy

When we respond to the whisper of God to obey Him in extravagant devotion, remarkable things happen. Sometimes, He directs us in paths that challenge us to the core, and often He bestows amazing joy. When people hear my stories about no salary and no home, they often get the wrong impression. They think these choices were easy for my family and me. They weren't. They were excruciating, but God used them in astounding ways.

The week after I told the church in Pine Bluff that I would forego my salary for the next year, I attended a pastor's meeting in Little Rock. To generate some cash, I had already sold my nice truck and bought an old Ford Bronco with almost 200,000 miles on it. When I arrived at our meeting, I was embarrassed about my vehicle and wanted to park as far away as possible, but the only available spot was near the entrance—right where the other men were walking into the building. It seemed each of them drove cars and trucks that looked fresh off the showroom floor. I was thoroughly ashamed of the hulk I was driving. As if to underscore my humiliation, the Bronco backfired as I pulled in. In my mind, the noise announced to everyone that the big loser had arrived!

> I knew it *shouldn't* matter what I drove, but it *did* matter!

For weeks, I'd been wrestling with all the material implications of my salary decision, but at that moment, I came face to face with the evil desire in my heart to look good in front of my peers. I even knew better. I knew it *shouldn't* matter what I drove, but it *did* matter! And I was hopping mad at God for leading me to do something so crazy. Then I was mad at myself because my concern about what other people thought mattered too much to me. Some humble servant of the Most High I turned out to be! As I stepped out of my Bronco and joined the assembly, I was just sure all the other pastors were secretly laughing at me. I was miserable.

I walked into the meeting room, preferring to remain anonymous at the moment, but the denominational superintendent came up to me. "Bryan, I know what's going on in your life. Is there anything you'd like to say to the rest of us?"

My heart sank even lower at his invitation to speak to the group. He probably thought I would describe God's glorious leading in my life and my rapturous joy in obeying the Master, but instead I spewed my anger, doubts, and

217

sin. I dumped a whole Bronco-load of my materialism and selfishness, and then I repented, right there in front of everyone.

The response of the men in the room astonished me. I had hoped at the least that they wouldn't laugh at me, but instead, they began to confess their own sins of material-ism. One pastor jumped to his feet and ran out of the room. When he came back a few minutes later, he explained that he had bought a motorcycle even though he knew God didn't want him to. Now, he was repenting, and he had stepped out to go list it for sale online. Another pastor admitted that he had lied at a denominational meeting to impress other pastors about the size of his church.

> I repented, right there in front of everyone.

218

Emotionally exhausted from my public display, I returned to my seat, dropped my head on the table, wept, and prayed. I paid no attention as, one by one, the other pastors confessed sins and repented before the group. Minutes, maybe hours, passed before I realized everyone had finished speaking. The room was quiet when I finally raised my head to look around. On the table in front of me was an enormous pile of cash and checks. God had led the men to pour out their hearts to Him and each other and to pour out their wallets for my family. Most were small church pastors whose salaries were very modest. Some were bi-vocational ministers who worked hard just to make ends meet each month. But each one gave out of the abundance of his heart. It was one of the most moving experiences of my life.

The next week, one of the pastors confessed to his church in Heber Springs, Arkansas the hold materialism had on his life. In his sermon, Pastor Tommy told my story and the impact it had on him. After his message, a man in pinstriped overalls stood up and announced, "We can't let that preacher starve!"

Tommy asked the man, "Well, what do you want us to do?"

He responded, "We need to take up an offering for him, Pastor."

The congregation had already taken up the weekly offering and the plates had been taken to another room. So they literally passed hats around the room. When the money was counted, that little church had collected $5,000 for Haley, me, and our family!

A young teenager named Benjamin Wilson was in the service that day in Heber Springs, and in the middle of the second offering, he bolted from the church. No one knew what he was doing or where he was going. When he got back to the church later that day, everyone had gone home, but he knocked at Pastor Tommy's office. As Tommy opened the door, Benjamin held out a cigar box containing about $200. It was every penny Benjamin had saved since he was a child.

"I have to give this to that pastor," he explained. "Would you make sure he gets it?"

A few days later, Tommy and his wife drove two hours to Pine Bluff to give me the $5,000 his people had given for us and Benjamin's cigar box. I still have that young man's box, with the money inside. The gift reminded me of a biblical story of King David. While away on a military campaign, he exclaimed to his men that he was thirsty for water from the well in Jerusalem. Wanting to serve their leader, several of his warriors sneaked across enemy lines to fulfill David's wish. When they gave the king the precious water, he was so moved by their love and generosity that he couldn't drink it. The offering from his men was too holy a sacrifice for him to merely quench his thirst with the water. He honored his soldiers by pouring it out as an offering to the God whom they all served. In the same way, I'll always keep this box as a memorial of God moving in the hearts of people in general—and one generous youth in particular—to provide for me.

Extreme?

Some people hear my stories and read about my response to God's extravagant love and think, "Man, that guy's nuts. What an extremist!"

A person's perspective depends on where he or she is standing. From the point of view of the typical American church, a life of extravagant devotion to Christ looks extreme. Most of us are far more interested in what God can do for us than in emptying alabaster jars of perfume as an expression of our pure, unfiltered gratitude for what He's already done for us. A life of complete trust, uncommon obedience, courageous faith, and outrageous generosity, though, is the only reasonable response to the matchless grace of God. Because God rescued us from sin and hell, we love Him with all our hearts, and we learn to love others with selfless kindness and patience. Because we have tasted the goodness of the Lord, sweet surrender to Him makes perfect sense. When we discern Him inviting us to deny our sinful desires, pick up our crosses and follow Him, we realize He's leading us to the only life worth living.

God wants us to live with open hands and thankful hearts. On the way to fulfilling His plans for us, He leads through cycles of sacrifice and blessing. At this point in my family's life, we live in an exquisite home. We enjoy every minute of it, but our past experiences of listening to God's whispered invitation to give it all reminds Haley and me that we actually don't own anything. We are temporary stewards of any possession God has given us, and we hold those things very loosely. Every day, we remember that all of our dollars and doorknobs are tools in the hands of God to shape us and touch the lives of others. We daily listen for His whispered instructions on how to use what He has entrusted to us for His glory and to build His kingdom.

If you've made it to the end of this book, you've shown your thirst for God. You haven't arrived at this point by luck or by coincidence. You had a divine appointment to read my stories and reflections on Scripture, answer some pointed questions, and reflect with friends about the importance of extravagant devotion. The word of God calls for a response, and you,

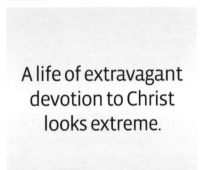

A life of extravagant devotion to Christ looks extreme.

by your diligence in reading and reflecting, have responded to Him with a resounding "Yes!"

Maybe you've already seen the pattern of command, obedience, and God's miraculous work in your life, or perhaps you realize it's time to set those spiritual gears in motion. So the question becomes: What is the next step of uncommon obedience for you? Do you need to make that phone call to an estranged family member to ask or offer forgiveness and begin a process of reconciliation? Is it time to step up and lead a small group or serve in a ministry? Do you need to confess your sin of materialism or the idolatry of putting something or someone in the place of God in your life? Have you been holding back your tithe and missions offerings because you didn't trust God to bless you financially if you give as He directs? Has God been calling you to leave the business world to become a pastor or a missionary, but so far you've come up with a hundred excuses? Do you need to let go of the security you feel in your job and start the business God is prompting you toward? Is it time to change the pattern of communication in your family from blame to kindness, and from demands to listening?

God waits on the hillside for people of simple faith and limited resources to offer Him a sack lunch so He can bless and multiply it. Each of us has a meal to offer of time, talents, and treasure. It may be all we have—that's what makes giving it an extravagant act—but when we do the simple deed of giving it to Him, He'll work miracles and touch other lives through us. Keep on learning the language of extravagance, and listen for the whisper of God. He will lead you to an act of extravagant devotion that will propel you to a new level of living, loving, learning, and leading.

> God wants us to live with open hands and thankful hearts.

Remember, remember, remember: Extravagant devotion captures the heart of God and unleashes His power and grace. From the days of Abraham through King David to Mary of Bethany to now, it always has.

Theirs did.

Mine does.

Yours will, too.

Think Outside the Box

1. *When have you heard God's voice and felt His nudge most clearly? What are some distractions that need to be cleared away so you can hear Him even better?*
2. *What principles or stories in this book have inspired, challenged, or threatened you the most? How can you put them into practice in your life?*

222

3. *Chapter 14 is called "Go and Do Likewise?" What is God saying to you about how to devote yourself extravagantly to Him? What do you need to go and do?*
4. *What can you do to cultivate a consistent lifestyle of devotion to God?*
5. *Why is offering extravagant devotion to God not really "extreme"?*

appendix A

how to use this book in classes and groups

Besides being a (hopefully) challenging and inspiring read for you as an individual, this book is designed for individual study, small groups, and classes. The best way to absorb and apply these principles is for participants to read on their own and answer the questions at the end of each chapter, then to discuss their answers in either a class or a group environment.

Each chapter's questions are designed to promote reflection, application, and discussion, so order enough copies for everyone to have a book. For couples, encourage both to have their own book so they can record their individual reflections.

The book is structured with 18 chapters to give you as a leader the flexibility in how long a group study can take. If you have the time, go through one chapter a week for 18 weeks. If time is in short supply (not an uncommon problem), you can make a six-week study out of it by covering three chapters each time you meet. The schedule below assumes six sessions, but you can adapt it as needed.

Week 1: Introduction to the Material
As the group leader, tell your own story, share hopes for the group, and provide books for each person. Encourage people to read the assigned chapter(s) each week and answer the questions before the next meeting.

Weeks 2-6: Introduce the Topic for the Week

In small groups, lead people through a discussion of the questions at the end of the chapters. In classes, teach the principles in each chapter, using personal illustrations, and inviting discussion. Share a story of how God has used the principles in your life.

Personalize Each Lesson

Don't feel pressured to cover every question in your group discussions. Pick out three or four that had the biggest impact on you, and focus on those, or ask people in the group to share their responses to the questions that meant the most to them that week.

Make sure you personalize the principles and applications. At least once in each group meeting, add your own story to illustrate a particular point.

Make the Scriptures come alive. Far too often, we read the Bible like it's a phone book, with little or no emotion. Paint a vivid picture for people. Provide insights about the context of people's encounters with God, and help those in your group sense the emotions of specific characters in each scene.

Focus on Application

The questions at the end of each chapter and your encouragement to be authentic will help your group take big steps toward applying the principles they're learning. Share how you are applying the principles in particular chapters each week, and encourage them to take steps of growth, too.

Three Types of Questions

If you've led groups before, you already understand the importance of asking open-ended (not "yes" or "no") questions to stimulate discussion. Three types of questions are *limiting, leading,* and *open.* Many of the questions at the end of each day's lessons are open questions.

- *Limiting questions* focus on an obvious answer, such as, "What does Jesus call Himself in John 10:11?" These don't stimulate reflection or discussion. If you want to use questions like this, follow them with thought-provoking open questions.
- *Leading questions* sometimes require the listener to guess what the leader has in mind, such as, "Why did Jesus use the metaphor of a shepherd in John 10?" (He was probably alluding to a passage in Ezekiel, but most people wouldn't know that.) The teacher who asks a leading question has a definite answer in mind. Instead of asking this question, he or she should teach the point and perhaps ask an open question about the point being made.
- *Open questions* usually don't have right or wrong answers. They stimulate thinking and are less threatening than the other types because the person answering doesn't risk being wrong. These questions often begin with "Why do you think...?" or "What are some reasons that...?" or "How would you have felt in that situation?"

Preparation

As you prepare to teach this material in a group or class, consider these steps:

1. *Carefully and thoughtfully read the book. Make notes, highlight key sections, quotes, or stories, and complete the reflection sections at the end of each chapter.*

This will familiarize you with the entire scope of the content.

2. *As you prepare for each week's session, re-read the corresponding chapters and make additional notes.*

3. *Tailor the amount of content to the time allotted. You won't have time to cover all the questions, so pick the ones that are most pertinent.*

4. *Pre-plan your own stories to personalize the message and add impact.*

5. *Before and during your preparation, ask God to give you wisdom, clarity, and power. Trust Him to use your group to change people's lives.*

6. *Most people will get far more out of the group if they read the chapters and complete the reflection each week. Order books before the group or class begins or after the first week.*

To Order More Copies of This Book
Extravagant is available online at
www.InfluenceResources.com
where group discounts are available. You can also buy this
book at most Christian bookstores.